Soulwinning
OUT WHERE THE PEOPLE ARE

by
T. L. Osborn

HARRISON HOUSE
Tulsa, Oklahoma

Soulwinning

OUT WHERE THE PEOPLE ARE

DEDICATED

TO DAISY, my companion in life and Associate Minister in evangelism in nearly 70 nations, who shares my belief that all human persons are created in God's image and therefore have infinite value and limitless potential for good, once they have the opportunity to understand God's LOVE-PLAN for them and to receive Jesus Christ into their lives.

T. L. Osborn

Bible quotations in this book have been personalized to encourage individual application. They are derived from King James Version unless otherwise noted. *(The Author)*

ISBN 0-89274-186-4
Copyright 1980 by T.L. Osborn
Printed in the United States of America

Contents

Osborn Crusade — Lubumbashi

Preface

A prominent soulwinner once said: "Let the cross be raised again at the center of the marketplace, as well as on the steeple of the church.

"Jesus was not crucified in a cathedral between two candles, but on a cross between two thieves — on the town heap, at the crossroads — so cosmopolitan that they had to write His title in Hebrew and Latin and Greek.

"The Son of God was crucified at the kind of place where cynics talk smut, where thieves curse, and where soldiers gamble.

"Because that is where Christ died and, since that is what He died about, that is where Christians can best share His message of love because **that is what real Christianity is all about.**"

***

From my conversion as a youth, I wanted to be a soulwinner. With a toy printing press, I printed scripture verses on little scraps of paper and distributed them.

Never did I dream that in a few years we would be publishing gospel literature in over 120 languages, at the rate of more than a ton per working day to facilitate personal soulwinning worldwide.

In the book of Acts there were only two methods of evangelism: **mass** evangelism and **personal** evangelism.

Within a short time after the death of the apostles, theological controversy usurped the place of soulwinning in the church and apostasy resulted. By the 4th century, the Dark Ages had already begun.

It was not until the 18th century that **mass** evangelism began to reappear under John Wesley. **Personal** evangelism as the early church practiced has only begun to be rediscovered.

For generations, Christians evangelized the church, the classrooms, the pews — but not the world. People were enlisted for the class or the club and invited to the church building where, it was hoped, they would decide for Christ. That was good for those few who would attend; but 90% of the unconverted never enter a church, so they can never be won there.

This is why the Christian's greatest opportunity is **outside** the church.

This book encourages and teaches Christians to win souls — at the factory, in the parks, on the streets, in the homes.

The Christian's greatest opportunity is not witnessing **inside** the church building, but **out in the world — out where the people are.**

The Church was born in a blaze of personal soulwinning. It was a house-to-house, face-to-face ministry.

This book on soulwinning is a stimulant for pastors and lay people to rekindle the individual Christian's passion for souls. It can serve as a passport to the busy crossroads and marketplaces of humanity — **out where the people are!**

Over 100,000 complimentary copies of the first edition of *Soulwinning* and its companion book were mailed to pastors, missionaries, national church leaders, and evangelists worldwide.

Its seed-concepts have helped produce a new breed of Jesus-followers around the world, promoting contact between church

INsiders and world OUTsiders in homes and schools, in factories and markets, in parks and streets — **out where humanity hurts most and only Christ's love can heal.**

These inspiring ideas met with such worldwide enthusiasm that we published a natural sequel, *Join This Chariot*.

Today, these two books are translated into many major languages and have already become **classics** in evangelism literature.

A fresh breeze of New Testament style evangelism is blowing across the world. The Christian's life motto is very simple:

One Way! One Job!

The **One Way** is Jesus!

The **One Job** is soulwinning!

There is no fulfillment like being part of God's number one job: giving the Good News to every creature, **winning souls — out where the people are!**

— T. L. Osborn

Soulwinning

OUT WHERE THE PEOPLE ARE

Osborn Crusade — The Hague

1
The Heartbeat Of Soulwinning

A group of Christian women were holding their regular prayer meeting.

The evangelist at their church, an ardent soulwinner, was their guest speaker.

He had overheard them talking about a disreputable woman in their neighborhood.

The evangelist asked them, "What are you doing to show Jesus' love to that lady?"

The leader spoke up, "We're faithfully praying for her salvation every time we meet."

"Fine," the evangelist remarked. "But she'll go to hell if **all** you do is pray for her. Have you gone to her? Have you shown Jesus' love to her? Have you gone to her home?"

The Errand Boy Philosophy
Have we made an errand boy out of God? Have we forgotten that He is the

Master and we are the servants? Do we tell God to do all the things which **we** are encouraged to do as Christian believers — visit the poor and needy, comfort the feeble, bless and provide for the destitute, encourage those in prison, sustain the weak, witness to unbelievers? Do we want God to do all of these things while we just pray?

Have we developed a religion of convenience?

Ponder this question: Can you think of one thing which Jesus Christ can do in your town or community without a body to operate through?

When God visited humankind to show Himself, He came in a physical body. Jesus Christ was God in the flesh. (See John 1:14; 2 Cor. 5:19.)

They killed Him but He returned in the form of the Holy Spirit to take up His abode in **our** bodies as His temple. (See 1 Cor. 6:19.)

Now, you and I are His body.

You are the church — the body of Christ today. **You** are Christ's body in your community.

Christ ministers through His body

today the same as He ministered through a human body some 2000 years ago. Today His body is the church. The church is **me** — my body, and **you** — your body. **We are His temple.**

I am the church. **I** am Christ's body.

You are the church. **You** are Christ's body.

For we are members of his body, of his flesh, and of his bones (Eph. 5:30).

Christ can do nothing, except through the church — His body. **That is you and me.** Not our congregation or our denomination, but **the church.** Christ's body is **me** and it is **you** — if you are a Christian.

When we stand before God, we will give an account of the deeds we personally have done. We will not be judged in the light of what our church did as a spiritual body. God will not call our assembly as a unit for judgment. He will not judge what our congregation has done as a part of the "corporate" body of Christ.

We will not be able to say, "Lord, my pastor will speak for me. I am a faithful member of the church body. We all work as a unit; therefore, I cannot answer as an individual."

As far as God is concerned, **you** personally are the church; **you** are Christ's body.

We talk about the church or body of Christ as being the mystical **union of believers** — the spiritual **community of called-out ones**. This is true. But like all truth, it must become personal. Otherwise, it is fruitless.

Christians usually regard the body of Christ in its general, collective sense — not in its personal application. Salvation is personal. Christ must live in us personally.

The great mystery which has been hid from ages and from generations, but now is made manifest to his saints ... is Christ in you! (Col. 1:26,27)

Christ **must** have a body to minister through. **That body is me — and you. We are the church — His body, His temple.**

This does not imply that we ignore the body of Christ in its collective, or so-called corporate sense, made up of all true believers. It means that you and I are alert to the fact that Jesus Christ is born in us and that **we are now His body**.

It sounds more correct to say, **We are members of his body** — and we are (1 Cor. 12:27). But this historic **membership** concept has somehow sedated the personal aspect of **Christ in you**.

Christians often remain devitalized in their churches, leaving the ministry to the community of believers. They say, "The church, the Sunday school, the ladies' society, the men's group, the youth teams — they will do it."

The members like to know that their church is doing things. They are willing to pay for this as long as some other member does the job.

But Christianity is a personal thing. If Christ has come to dwell in you, **you are His body** — that is, so far as you are concerned. He dwells in you because He wills to minister **through you**. He must have **your body** in order to reach **your community**. The essence of your Christian experience is *"Christ in you."*

When He was in Nazareth, *He could do no mighty work there ... because of*

their unbelief (Mark 6:5,6). Without
human faith on the part of the people,
His ministry was limited then. Without
humans as instruments to live and speak
through, He is limited today.

God Could Have Sent Angels

How often it has been said, "God
could have sent angels to preach this gospel, but He did not. He has ordained that
human beings preach it. If they do not, it
shall not be proclaimed — and souls
shall be lost."

**The preaching of the gospel is lim-
ited to the willingness of human persons to step forth and open their
mouths for Him to speak through.**

This same fact applies to **all** phases of
Christian living and witnessing.

Christ cannot visit the encarcerated
unless He can go in **your body**. He will
go **in you**. **You** are the church. When
you visit those in prison, Christ is visiting them **through you**. Otherwise, He
cannot.

Through the tradition of prayer, have
we made an errand boy out of God?

Prayer is vital to a Christian. Christ

taught us to pray but He told us what to pray for. Christ prayed but He did more than pray. *He went about doing good* (Acts 10:38), witnessing, comforting, visiting, speaking, showing compassion, **demonstrating God in action.**

How sacred we make our traditional prayers sound. How humble and how dedicated we feel while we are at prayer, sending God all of our orders for the day or week.

Do we tell Him to do the things which **we**, as Christians are encouraged to do? Shall we just tell Him to preach, too? If He is so convenient for us, would He mind including some preaching now and then, on our behalf?

With Us, But Now In Us

Isn't it strange: We talk about how the Spirit was **with** people before Pentecost. Now we rejoice that He is **in** us.

That is exactly where He is — **in** us. Not floating around the world, hovering over human beings here and there as they direct Him — solving their problems, visiting and encouraging people — while we live our quiet, personal lives in privacy.

Through God's redemptive plan, Jesus Christ has now returned through the Holy Spirit to live and act THROUGH US.

Now Christ is born in us!

For God is at work within you, helping you want to obey Him, and then helping you do what He wants (Phil. 2:13 L.B.). This is what God did in Christ. Now He does the same in us because **we** are His body.

He speaks through **our** lips.

He visits the needy and uplifts the fallen **through us**.

He encourages the discouraged and reaches down to the despondent **through us**.

He heals the brokenhearted and binds up the wounds of the suffering **through us. You and I are His body.** We are the church.

Now you can understand why the evangelist told the ladies' prayer group: "That woman will go to hell if **all** you do is pray for her."

If we fail to do more than pray — if we never visit the lost and witness to people — they will never hear Christ's invitation to be saved. We must pray, but then we must **arise, go out, and give them the good news**.

The Gospel In Your Community

Christ's ministry in your community is expressed **through you**.

He longs to speak to people about salvation, to convince them of their sins and of the gospel, which is the work of the Holy Spirit.

But He is **in you** and He works **through your lips** and **your body**. If you do not go and witness or speak the message, your community may be lost. Christ's plan is to live in you and He cannot visit people independent of you — no more than He can stand in the public place and preach the gospel without a Christian to speak through.

Do we prefer to live selfishly ... to get alone and pray, sending up a barrage of orders and errands for the wonderful Holy Spirit to move around and do for us? Are we too busy with our TV programs, our clubs, our recreational activities, our other private interests?

He Has No Other Channel

Let us remember that the Holy Spirit moves **through us**. We are His temple. **If we are too busy to witness, He has no other channel through which to minister.** He lives in our bodies.

Non-Christians in your community will **never** be visited by our Lord if you do not go and speak to them in His name.

Those who are sick and in prison shall never be visited by Jesus Christ if you do not go to them in His name.

People shall never see God, except as they see Him **in you**.

Christ's love can only be manifested through the life of a believer. His compassion and concern for lost souls can only be exhibited **through you**.

Jesus Christ visits your community each time **you** do.

Are you unwittingly confining Him to your house?

Do you ever let Him speak to your neighbors?

Have you ever allowed Him to tell them the way of salvation and to offer them His life?

Do you accuse them of living in false-
hood, while neglecting to let Jesus Christ
tell them the truth?

The Church — Christ's Body —
Is YOU

Have you always thought these things
are the responsibility of the church? You
are absolutely right. They are.

However, the church is **not** the congregation or a denomination. The church
is Christ's body, **and that is what you
are!**

Christ does not live in a cathedral of
stone or in a temple of brick and mortar.
He lives in **your** body. **You** are His temple. He ministers, exhibits Himself, dem-
onstrates His compassion, extends His
mercy through **your** body — through
you!

This truth is the heartbeat, the pulse,
the motivation, of personal soulwinning.
Everything else constitutes the mere
mechanics of personal witnessing. This
truth comprises the essence, the spirit,
the **dynamics** of personal witnessing.

Mechanics or Dynamics

You can memorize the **mechanics**. But the **dynamics** must be born in you. It must be a divine revelation — a miracle.

That spiritual miracle is taking place in you right now as you read, so that personal soulwinning will have a new life-giving dimension in and through your life.

You have been saved to be His witness, His body, His church, His voice, His heartbeat.

Your body has become His temple. He ministers **through you**. You are lost in Him. His life is the energy of your witness. You go on His behalf so that He can go **through you** and reach the unconverted.

That is Christianity in depth! Everything else is superficial and without significance. Christ is in you. You have a purpose for living and witnessing.

A soulwinner visited a Sunday School and was asked to teach a large class.

He asked, "How many here are Christians?"

Everyone raised his or her hands and the regular teacher exulted, "Wonderful!"

But the guest teacher countered, "No, it's terrible! We should have unbelievers here and get them converted in this classroom."

He was correct.

Often the church — what we refer to as the church, is segregated from the unconverted. It has been called "the sacred spot where little groups meet to minister to themselves in seclusion."

Quietly Learning Of Christ In Depth

As an evangelist tried to arouse a small congregation in Japan to be more evangelistic, the pastor said, "You don't understand. We don't want a large crowd. We only want a small group which can meet together in quietness to study the Word and learn of Christ in depth."

An evangelist spoke to a men's prayer group about going out to witness for Christ from house to house.

The leader responded, "We can't do that. We're not deep enough in God."

"How long have you been meeting and praying?" asked the evangelist.

"Only two years."

For two years they had kept their Lord confined to a room and had never allowed Him to share His life with people in their community.

What a contrast with Christians in the early church! In just two years, they made the Word of the Lord heard by *all who dwelt in Asia* (Acts 19:10).

The reason the gospel has not been preached *to every creature* is because individual Christians have misunderstood **who** the church really is.

It is correct to speak of the church as the collective body of Christians; but from a personal standpoint, the church is **you! Your** body is Christ's body. He can only witness and minister **through you and through me.**

Christians have misinterpreted the Holy Spirit and His ministry through them.

Could this be why the world is not yet evangelized?

Might this explain why unconverted people sometimes ridicule the church and Christians?

Is this a clue to why communists mock Christianity?

Is this one reason why the Jews reject Christianity? Their leaders read the New Testament and know who Jesus was — that He was a Jew. They know how He lived and how He told His followers to live. But they also know how differently most Christians today live, by comparison.

Jesus was a soulwinner. He ·mixed with people. He befriended the needy, healed the sick, spoke good news to people. He was servant to the people, all the time.

Has He ever changed? Does He will to do the same today? He works in you *both desiring and doing his good pleasure* (Phil. 2:13). But can He do these same things today if you and I do not allow Him to, through our bodies? **Without our bodies to express Himself through, is not Jesus cut off from people?**

The Director Of Evangelism

There was a man who had directed the evangelism department of a large church. The new pastor was a zealous soulwinner. Soon after he was elected, he took the evangelism director with him in door-to-door witnessing.

When they returned that night after leading several souls to Christ, he said to the pastor, "I've directed the ministry of evangelism in this church for 33 years. But tonight, I have a personal knowledge of Jesus Christ that I now realize I have never experienced before."

Love For Those Who Hurt

A lady who was a faithful member of a church became involved with a married man. When it was discovered, she was ashamed. So she left the church, purposing never to return.

The ladies' society met and prayed for her. But then they did more. They delegated one of their group to go to their friend and express their love and concern for her. This was the Spirit of the Good Shepherd at work in those women. (See Matt. 18:11,12.)

All day long, the Christian sought for the woman but could not find her. She set out again early the next day and at noon found her alone and depressed.

"Come back to church," she said.

"I can never return," replied the hurting woman.

"But we **want** you to come!"

"Do the women **want** me?"

"Yes, they sent me to assure you that **we love you. We want you**."

The lady returned to those who loved her and was forgiven, reinstated and encouraged in the name of Christ.

This happened because a Christian woman did what Jesus wants to do. She let Him seek out the one who had strayed from the fold. **He did it through her!**

This is real Christianity!

At first, you may be afraid or timid or hesitant to act in Christ's stead, but go in His name. **He is in you.** Yield your emotions to Him. He will guide you and you will discover a dimension in Christian living you never knew before.

Some ask, "How can I know when God is speaking to me and leading me to do something?"

It's very simple. I explain it like this: Listen, and you will hear! Look, and you will see! Reach out and you will touch!

You will know God's voice. Then just **act** on the ideas you receive that will help

and lift people and that will bring glory
to God.

What voice would tell you to go share
Jesus Christ and His love with someone?
To lift or help or heal or forgive some-
one?

The Witness At Midnight

After attending church one night, a
certain Christian could not go to sleep.
He felt impressed to talk to a man about
Christ's love for him.

Finally, after midnight, he arose,
dressed, and went to the man's house.
When he knocked, the man came to the
door at once.

The Christian apologized, "It looks
foolish for me to be knocking on your
door at such an hour."

"Not at all!" came the quick reply.

"I've had no rest. I feel I must get
right with God and I need help. You are
the very man I wanted to speak to,
because I have confidence in your life."

The man was born again that night!

**You will grow deepest in Christ by
sharing Him.** He will become more real
to you than ever before, as He ministers

through your body — through YOU, His church, His temple.

This truth, therefore, is the very heartbeat of Christian living and of soul-winning.

T.L. Osborn teaching at international convention in Texas.

2
Let's Take A Journey

How would you like to visit the early church?

Would their lifestyle of soulwinning interest you? How do you think they went about it? Who were the preachers? How many were witnesses? What denomination was the largest or the most popular?

What is your personal concept of the church in New Testament times? Could we follow its example, or have times changed too much?

Let's take a journey in our minds back to those churches. Stopping at the church at Ephesus, let's imagine a conversation we might have:

"Good evening, Aquila. We understand you're a member of the church here. Could we come in and visit for awhile?"

"Certainly. Come in."

"If you don't mind, we would like for you to tell us about the way the churches here in Asia Minor carry on their soulwinning program. We read that you have been a member of a church in Corinth and Rome, as well as this one here in Ephesus. You should be very well qualified to tell us about evangelism in the New Testament church. If you don't mind, we'd like to visit your church while we're here."

"Sit down. You're already in the church. It meets here in my home."

"You don't have a church building?"

"What's a church building? No, I guess we don't."

"Tell me, Aquila, what is your church doing to evangelize Ephesus? What are you doing to reach the city with the gospel?"

"Oh, we've already evangelized Ephesus. Every person in the city clearly understands the gospel."

"What?"

"Yes. Is that unusual?"

"How did the church do it? You certainly don't have radio, television, or electronic communication. Did you have a lot of evangelistic campaigns?"

"No. As you have probably heard, we tried mass meetings in this area, but most of the time we would end up in jail."

"Then how?"

"We just went to every home in the city. That's the way the church in Jerusalem first evangelized that city.[1] The disciples there evangelized the entire city of Jerusalem in a very short time. All the other churches in Asia Minor have followed their example."

"Is it effective everywhere?"

"Yes, it is. There are so many converts that some of the pagan leaders fear their own religions will die. When Paul left Ephesus for the last time, he reminded us to keep on following this same procedure."[2]

"Aquila, this is amazing! At this rate, there is no telling how many people are going to hear the gospel and respond."

"Oh, haven't you heard? We've already shared the gospel with every person in Asia Minor, both Jews and Greeks."[3]

[1]Acts 5:42
[2]Acts 20:20
[3]Acts 19:10

"That's not possible. You can't mean everyone!"

"Yes, everyone."

"But that would include Damascus, Ephesus, dozens of large cities, as well as towns and villages. What about the nomadic tribes on the desert? How long did it take the churches to reach all of these people?"

"Not long; 24 months to be exact.[3] The same thing is happening in North Africa and Southern Europe. The gospel has reached Spain, too. We've heard of a land called England, and several Christians may be there by now."

"Aquila, what you're telling us is incredible. You have done more in one generation than we have done in a thousand years!"

"That's strange. It's been rather simple for us to do. It's hard to realize things have moved so slowly for you. Maybe there is a better way to spread the Good News."

Osborn Crusade — Enugu

Mobile Units equipped with projectors, generators, miracle films, screens, gospel tapes, players and stockpiles of tracts are provided FREE to missions worldwide by the Osborn Ministries — for SOULWINNING.

3
Born in a Blaze

I was only twelve years old when I was converted, but from that day, I wanted to be a soulwinner.

I was the seventh son of my parents. My father was the seventh son of his parents. I was raised on a farm and worked hard.

An older brother was converted at an old fashioned brush arbor meeting. There was such a great change in him that, even as a twelve-year-old boy, I became very interested. Lonnie, my brother, took me to a revival meeting in an old building at Mannford, Oklahoma.

That night I received Jesus Christ as my Savior and became His follower.

Within a few months my father moved us into town. He opened a feed mill and an agency to buy dairy cream on behalf of a large company. I operated the cream station.

With a toy printing press, I printed scripture verses on scraps of paper — my first tracts, and distributed them among the townspeople. The population was only about 350. Little did I dream that in a few years we would be publishing gospel literature in more than 120 languages at a rate of more than a ton per working day.

From the time I was converted, I had one simple, basic desire: I wanted to be a **real** soulwinner.

Years have come and gone now. I started preaching at age fifteen, married at eighteen, became a missionary in India at twenty-one. We have preached face to face to millions of people in nearly seventy countries.

The more my wife, Daisy, and I study the scriptures and the further we travel in evangelism, the more we are convinced of this fact: **The greatest calling for every Christian is to lead people to Christ.**

In this book, I share *Seven Reasons Why We Are Soulwinners*. These chapters present many new ideas for pastors, new concepts for Christians, new inspiration for evangelists, new goals for churches. This may be the most vital book for believers with a passion for souls that we have ever published.

Unbelieveable as it may seem, the first book ever written on personal soul-winning was published since 1900.

Many Christians, pastors, and churches have not yet rediscovered the powerful ministry of **witnessing out where the people are** — as the early church did.

Two Kinds Of Evangelism

In the book of Acts there were only two types of evangelism practiced: **mass evangelism** and **personal evangelism**. By far, the greatest results were achieved through the latter.

The early church was born in a blaze of personal witnessing about Jesus Christ.

Occasionally, multitudes assembled to hear one of those Christians speak, especially where some outstanding healing miracle had occurred. Consistently, those carly believers were busy in market-places, on the streets, in the houses, persuading men and women to believe on Jesus Christ.

They were **personal soulwinners!**

The first chapter of Acts begins with the standard for the early Christians. What *Jesus began both to do and teach* when He walked on earth, He *continued* doing and teaching through them. He was living and ministering through them — and they knew it. They were His voice, His feet, His body. He was carrying on what He *began* and He was doing it through them.

The Bible makes some fantastic statements about their success. *Daily in the temple, and in every house, they never stopped teaching and preaching Jesus Christ* (Acts 5:42).

The Perfect 20-20 Vision

Those early Christians had "20-20" vision: Acts 20:20. *I ... have taught you publicly, and from house to house, testifying both to the Jews, and also to the Greeks, repentance toward God, and faith toward our Lord Jesus Christ.*

Here we see them engaged in the two types of evangelism:

Mass evangelism — *taught publicly.*

Personal evangelism — *from house to house.*

From Acts chapter 2 until Acts chapter 20 (about thirty years), door-to-door soulwinning was their lifestyle.

Tucked away in chapter 19 is one of the most exciting verses: *This continued for two years; so that everyone who lived in Asia heard the word of the Lord Jesus, both Jews and Greeks* (Acts 19:10).

Think of it! In two years, all Asia Minor heard the gospel. And it was done without automobiles, jet planes, radio, TV, tapes, records, films, videos or newspapers. It was done through **mass evangelism** and **personal evangelism**.

Why were the 1st century Christians able to accomplish so much when Christians in our time, with so many fantastic advantages, accomplish, by comparison, so much less?

Mainly because **personal soulwinning** — the most effective arm of New Testament evangelism — has not been practiced in the traditional church of this century.

A Brief History Of Evangelism

To explain why I say that, let me give you a brief review of the history of evangelism.

During the 1st century after Christ,
His followers possessed an unquenchable
passion and undying zeal to persuade
everyone about Christ. They remembered
His promise to return as soon as the gospel was *preached in all the world for a
witness to all nations* (Matt. 24:14).

Then in the 2nd century, Christianity
became entangled in theological controversy. Rather than pressing on to the *uttermost parts* and to the *regions beyond,*
they began to argue over doctrinal points.

The 3rd century found Christianity
sinking into apostasy.

The 4th century closed the gap —
their backsliding and compromise was
complete.

Christianity was then plunged into
1,000 years of spiritual darkness — the
Dark Ages. This terrible thousand years
has become a veil that has obstructed the
contemporary church from perceiving
New Testament methods.

Martin Luther first broke out of the
darkness with the revelation that *the just
shall live by faith* (Rom. 1:17). But the

reformation led by Luther, was not a return to **mass** and **personal soulwinning**. It was a revolt against the religious hierarchy and an invitation for believers to examine the scriptures for themselves — something forbidden by the ruling clergy.

Luther said practically nothing about missions or world evangelism. In fact, it was almost 1800 A.D. before William Carey brought the concept of missions back to the heart of believers.

The teachings on the baptism of the Holy Spirit were not rediscovered until the 20th century.

The Long Road Back

Christianity has endured a prolonged and tenacious resistance to New Testament concepts. Many have not yet returned to the foundation of the early church — the basic principle of **personal soulwinning** which is Christ ministering **through a believer**.

Mass evangelism reappeared about 200 years ago through John Wesley. Men like George Whitefield introduced it in the western hemisphere.

There have been about four peaks in **mass evangelism**: under Wesley, Finney, Moody, and — greatest of all — since the turn of the 20th century.

In the mid-1700's, a great moving of God's Spirit was manifested through what was called the camp meeting epoch.

In the 1800's, the brush arbor became popular.

Then revival became vogue. In the 20th century, the words revival and evangelism became intermingled. Later the popular terms varied between revival and evangelistic crusade or campaign, either church-centered or city-wide.

However, **personal evangelism** has not yet been generally rediscovered by the institutionalized church.

Torrey and Spurgeon wrote the first two books on personal evangelism early in the 20th century. Since then, hundreds and hundreds of books have been published on the subject. Unfortunately their content usually indicates that the New Testament concept of **personal soulwinning** has not yet been rediscovered by the popular membership of historical church organizations.

Many varieties of programs, projects, plans and crusades on "enlistment evangelism" have mushroomed.

The main emphasis has been to get unchurched people to Sunday School, to a Bible class, or to the church meetings.

Generally, little has been taught among denominations on how to actually win souls, how to lead people to a decision for Christ, how to reach them out where they are — **at the factories, restaurants, parks; on the streets; and in the homes of people.**

Too often Christians are not taught that each believer, as an individual, is Christ's body; that the Lord can only reach people **through individuals**; that **each believer is Christ's body on earth today!**

Many churches have excellent programs and training classes on how to invite people to church, but not on how to get them to accept Christ **out where they live, work and play**.

Reversing The Pattern

In the New Testament, they testified from *house to house* and made disciples among the people.

The traditional concept has been to get people to church first, then to Christ. This system is fine for those who will go to church, but about 90% of unbelievers never go.

The New Testament concept is to get people to Christ, then to the meeting place — **to win them out where they are.** There the possibilities are indeed limitless!

Most training programs have been based on recommending the church building. The New Testament concept was based on **recommending Christ**.

Whether or not we like to admit it, the church, as a building or denomination, has very little appeal to hurting people.

Yet the exciting fact is that **the person of Jesus Christ**, when presented correctly, **has the greatest single appeal to the human heart in this world.**

The Most Evangelized Acre

In his book, *How To Have A Soulwinning Church,* Gene Edwards says: "We have attempted to evangelize the world ... by evangelizing the church building ... each room and every pew. It has been the most evangelized acre on earth. The way we have worked at it, you would think the building needed converting. We have worked as though all the lost people in the world were there."

The only problem is that the unconverted, the masses of unsaved, have never been there and never will be there. They are everywhere except where we have been trying to get them to come — inside the church.

The opportunity therefore, is **to go out where the people are** and win them there. **Then** they will gladly come into the church.

After years of waiting in the wings, personal evangelism is finally making its re-entry into Christian history, commanding the center stage of many soulwinning organizations, and evangelistic churches and individuals.

Edwards, one who has strongly

advocated **personal soulwinning**, says:

"There has not been a time in the last 1800 years, when a great movement of personal witnessing has gripped a large portion of Christian people. Open your history books and turn back through nearly two millenniums. You will discover that the most powerful and necessary concept of Christianity has remained, until recent years, dead. We've had a car without a motor, a plane without wings.

"A revival — a rediscovery — of personal evangelism is, in truth, a rediscovery of the spirit of New Testament Christianity."

Mass evangelism reaches only those who attend the crusade. Church enlistment evangelism reaches only those who attend class or Sunday School or church.

Personal evangelism is the only way to reach **every** creature. It is not centered at the crusade or inside the church building. It is **outside — out where the people are.**

Church buildings — a vital asset to Christianity in any generation — were not a New Testament concept at all.

Again, I quote Gene Edwards:

"The church building concept of evangelism has been the greatest single hindrance to world evangelization — not because we have had church buildings, but because we have not gotten out of them."

Edwards even went so far as to say:

"A church building serves one purpose: to keep you warm in winter, cool in summer and dry when it rains.

"This is not an appeal for you to go burn down your church building, but to see it in its right perspective. Realize that evangelism is not to be centered inside the church building. The church is not a place to bring people into, to convert them. It is a refueling station — **to send Christians out from.**"

Segregated Societies

Just before Christ ascended, He plainly told His followers where to go and what to do in terms too clear to be confused.

But you shall receive power, after that the Holy Ghost is come upon you: and you shall be witnesses unto me both in

Jerusalem, and in all Judea, and in Samaria, and to the uttermost part of the earth (Acts 1:8).

Get your map and see what this means: *Jerusalem* is your hometown. *All Judea* represents your state or province or nation.

But why did He specify Samaria? It was part of Judea and He had already said *in all Judea.* I will tell you why He specified *and in Samaria.*

Samaria was segregated! *The Jews have no dealings with the Samaritans* (John 4:9). Remember when the Jews slandered Jesus: *Say we not well that you are a Samaritan, and have a devil?* (John 8:48).

Jesus told us to reach *all Judea;* then He repeated *and Samaria* — the forgotten, hurting, unloved masses.

Samaria can be Indian or Aboriginal reservations, minority communities, migrant settlements, ghettos, rehabilitation centers, immigrant and refugee communities or any place that is considered inferior or is segregated from the mainstream of society.

Jesus listed these places, then added,

And unto the uttermost part of the earth. In other words, He was saying, "At home and abroad." **Soulwinning is a world-wide ministry.**

The two types of evangelism — **mass** and **personal** — originated with the early church. My wife, Daisy, and I are following their example.

In **mass evangelism**, we have already preached to millions face to face. But regardless of the masses who attend our crusades, there are always millions of others in the same country who do not attend.

Mass evangelism can only reach the masses who attend. It can never reach the millions who do not choose to attend.

Radio and TV evangelism can only reach those fortunate ones who have a radio or a television set. It does not reach the multiplied millions who are too poor or too primitive to have access to these media.

The masses can only be reached by **personal evangelism**. A great percentage of these can actually be won to Christ through personal witnessing. Fortunately, 100% of those who are not won can at least be given a personal witness. It is the only way to reach *every creature*.

We are engaged in every possible concept of **mass evangelism**, to reach the largest possible number of those who can be attracted to a public gospel meeting.

We are involved in **personal evangelism** to reach those millions who will not attend a gospel crusade. We have developed and supply stockpiles of various soulwinning "tools" (tracts, books, tapes, films, videos) to both induce Christians to go out after souls and to help make their witness more effective when they do share the good news.

The early church had mass meetings occasionally. But, their greatest results were always effected through believers who were engaged in personal evangelism, winning people to Christ in face-to-face, house-to-house ministry. *And the Lord added to the church daily* (Acts 2:47).

Minimal Church Growth

Did you ever stop to think that the minimum number of converts in your church would be 365 souls per year if the Lord added to the church daily?

Yet there are very few churches in all of the world which achieve that minimal level of growth.

How did the early church do this?

The answer is found in Acts 20:20, as referred to previously in this chapter: They taught *publicly, and from house to house*.

That 20-20 vision still works today! That is what **is happening** where the principles shared in this book are being implemented.

Most pastors and Christians are concerned about their church. They wonder why the unconverted do not attend. They even pray for them to come. Usually they do not go out where the people are. If they just pray, the unconverted will be lost because Christ can only reach them **through the Christian's personal life and witness**.

Is it not expecting too much for non-Christians to come to the church buildings to receive Christ? Should not Christians allow Christ to visit the unconverted **wherever they are** — through His body, the church?

Are we expecting too much when we

ask Christians to go to the houses of
people — **out where they are?**

We are His body.

Moody Bible Institute has estimated
that less than 5% of Christians have ever
led a soul to Christ.

Only about 10% of the people in so-
called Christian nations attend church.

Sometimes I'm amazed to see God
getting more cooperation from non-
Christians than from Christians. There
are unbelievers who will come to
God's house, but there is a much smaller
percentage of Christians who will go
share Christ in non-Christian homes.

Of whom does God require the most?
He never said, "Go ye unconverted to
my house and be saved, lest ye die." But
He **did** say, *Go ye (believers) ... to every
creature*.

My wife, Daisy, and I feel that this is
our greatest opportunity. It is our call,
our ministry, our open door of service to
people. It is **your** opportunity too, **if** you
have believed on Jesus Christ. It is **your**
call too. Jesus Christ wants to witness to
people and to love them **through you**.

From The Gallery To The Arena

Personal soulwinning is the open door of success for every Christian on earth. It is the opportunity that transforms a Christian from being just a spectator, into a direct instrument of the Holy Spirit. It lifts believers out of the **gallery** of being only hearers of the word. Suddenly, they step out into the arena as *doers of the word* (James 1:22-25).

There is nothing as exciting as coming to church and looking across the aisle at a new believer you have personally led to Christ. **He did it through you.** You found the lost person out where the people are. You let Christ win that soul **through you.** No church can be ineffective when, scattered throughout its congregation are members like that.

This book is meant to encourage the methods of early Christianity — the soulwinning method, the house-to-house operation that inspires Christians to go out and to share Christ with people **wherever they are**.

The church was born in a blaze of personal soulwinning. In a revival of that passion, the church of Jesus Christ will reach her finest hour as believers write the church's last chapter before Christ's return.

To that end, I have outlined in this book *Seven Reasons Why We Are Soulwinners:*

1. *Because Jesus was.*
2. *Because the harvest is so great.*
3. *Because the laborers are so few.*
4. *Because Jesus said to do it.*
5. *Because of the unfulfilled prophecies concerning Christ's return.*
6. *Because we do not want the blood of non-Christians on our hands.*
7. *Because of what we have experienced.*

4
The Greatest Calling

Daisy, my wife, and I are soulwinners because Jesus was!

The Bible says: *This is a faithful saying, and worthy of all acceptation.*

What is this all important saying?

That Christ Jesus came into the world to save sinners (1 Tim. 1:15).

Luke 19:10 says, *The Son of man is come to seek and to save that which was lost.*

Jesus came to save people. That is His mission.

First and last, **Jesus was a soulwinner** — the greatest soulwinner the world has ever known!

The first group Jesus chose to follow Him received this challenge: *Follow me, and I will make you fishers of people* (Matt. 4:19).

The last group who followed Him out to His ascension received this command: *"You shall be my witnesses to the world. Go make disciples of all nations."*

First and foremost, Jesus was a soulwinner.

That is why He came: **to save people.**

That is why He lived, died, rose again, and sent the Holy Ghost to His followers: to make them effective soulwinners.

The word **Christian** means Christ-like. Christ came to save people, to seek out the lost; so to be **Christians**, we are to be soulwinners.

Christ is born in us and He wills to do the same things **in and through us** that He did when He walked on earth.

Yet, there are hundreds of thousands of Christians who have never known the joy of allowing Christ to win even one soul through them. There are even preachers and Bible teachers who have never won a soul to Christ.

Missionaries have confided in me that they had never won a soul to Christ during their entire term of ministry abroad.

I repeat: **To be a Christian means to be like Christ and to be like Christ is to be a soulwinner.**

Can this be the reason the church has not succeeded in giving the good news to *every creature?*

Have the majority of Christians not yet discovered this truth?

Since you are the church, since you are Christ's body in the earth, you can let Him win souls through you. You can be a vital instrument in meeting the spiritual need of your generation.

Jesus took His message **to the people**. He went **wherever the people were** — in the marketplaces, on street corners, on the mountain sides, by the seashores, in the homes.

He was criticized by the religious leaders for identifying with people, where they were. *This man receives sinners, and eats with them* (Luke 15:2).

He Walked With Sinners

Jesus mixed with people. He witnessed to them, convinced them, and won them. He was not a holier-than-thou type, a religious snob — aloof and sanctimonious. **He walked with people. They were His reason for being in this world.**

It can be that way with every Christian. To be Christlike means to win people. His purpose is our purpose. His mission is our mission. His plan is our plan. He came to save people. We are here in this world for the same purpose.

In John 18:37, He said, *For this cause I came into the world, to bear witness of the truth.* That is why we are in this world: to bear witness of the truth which is Jesus Christ. (See John 14:6.)

He encouraged us to *go out into the highways and hedges, and compel them to come in, that my house may be filled* (Luke 14:23).

He never said, "Go ring a church bell and pray for people to come in."

He said, "Go out and compel them. Win them, bring them in. You go out and get them, that my house may be full."

Every follower of His did just that.

After His ascension, Jesus' followers acted just like Him. They were busy witnessing in the markets, on the streets, in houses, around the public wells; talking, reasoning, witnessing, persuading, preaching, winning souls, compelling people to believe the gospel — just like Jesus did.

In fact, they reminded everyone so much of Christ that critics, with contempt in their voices, called them "CHRIST-i-ans." Their critics did not know that Christ was actually reborn in His followers. They imitated His way of life. They taught and lived and acted like Jesus Christ. They were like Him in winning souls.

That is why we are soulwinners: Because Jesus was!

The Bible says, *Daily in the temple, and in every house, they never stopped teaching and preaching Jesus Christ* (Acts 5:42).

In my New Testament, I have circled the word *daily.*

Today, many churches are open no more than twice or three times a week; while sports, cinemas, casinos, race tracks, bars, amusement parks and discos are doing business **daily**.

Too often the church building is only opened on Sunday. But the real church is **you and me**. **We are Christ's body.** Christ can minister and witness through us **every day** — regardless of whether or not the church building is open.

Early Christians were *daily* in the temple and in every house, teaching and preaching Jesus Christ.

Contemporary Witnessing

Christians who are becoming aware of these principles, are recapturing the zeal and passion of the early church, and are sharing the good news of Jesus Christ with others.

Did you know that the Jehovah's Witnesses have added more converts to their membership during this century than any religious body? While traditional churches were losing members, they were winning. Why?

One simple reason: From their inception, they exploited the most strategic secret of the early church and encouraged every convert to be a door-to-door witness.

While traditional Christians were using their **church pews**, the Jehovah's Witnesses were using their **shoe soles**. While church members beat a path **to the sanctuary**, the Jehovah's Witnesses beat a path **to the people** — and there they made converts.

When they meet in their kingdom halls, it is not to win converts. It is a meeting of those already converted.

There they gather to be instructed in witnessing. They master their doctrines. They are trained to be witnesses.

When they get ready to make converts, they go out to the streets, carrying a tape or cassette player and loaded with attractive literature. They systematically work each section of a town, street by street, knocking on doors, entering homes, witnessing, and winning — **out where the people are.**

In *Christianity Today,* one writer said, "How ever one may disagree with Jehovah's Witnesses or Mormons, we must admire the dedication and sense of mission that takes them from door to door in the face of ridicule and abuse."

Jehovah's Witnesses succeed because they stay at it.

A Hungry World

People are bewildered and confused about spiritual values. They are lost and they search for direction, but they do not trust the church for guidance. Too often they have not received a true witness of the gospel.

They are streaming to the psychologists and psychiatrists. They are the human guinea pigs for every new theory that is conceived by the growing wave of psychoanalysts.

Children are confused. Teenagers are adrift. Parents are bickering. Insecurity and dismay dominate the home. Drinking and perversion are substituted for stability in family life.

Sickness, disease, mental stress, and spiritual emptiness go unattended. Wretched existences constitute the life-style behind the doors of many of the affluent-appearing homes.

Through those doors is an open world of ministry for Christians, but millions of church members have never approached them.

We pray for people to be saved. Jesus said, *Go out and get them.* They will be lost while we pray. **Christ can only speak to them through us. We are His legs, His voice, His hands, His body.**

Today is the opportunity for Holy-Spirit-filled specialists in soulwinning.

Tradition has taught us that evangelists are soulwinners, but that everyone else ministers to those already saved.

First, A Christian

A pastor says, "Oh, I'm not a soul-winner. I never could deal with non-Christians. My calling is to pastor, to shepherd the flock."

Who was the greatest shepherd?

Jesus!

He was also the greatest soulwinner. If I were a pastor, I would want to follow His example.

Another person told me, "Oh, no! I do not make public invitations to accept Christ. That is not my calling. My gift is to teach."

Who was the greatest teacher?

Jesus!

He was also the world's greatest soul-winner. If I were a teacher, I would want to follow Christ's example of teaching in a way that I could convince people about Christ.

I am a soulwinner because Jesus was.

A preacher said to me: "Oh, reaching the unconverted is not my calling at all. My gift is to teach prophecy."

Who was the greatest prophet?

Jesus!

He was also a soulwinner.

A minister friend dared to say, "I teach types and shadows from the Old Testament. I'm not a soulwinner. I minister to the church."

Who did that better than Jesus? Yet He won souls when He taught.

What I am saying is: Before you were a pastor, you were a Christian — Christlike.

First, you are called as a Christian to win souls.

Then, you may be called to pastor or shepherd a flock.

Every pastor can be a soulwinner because that is what a Christian is — like Christ, and Jesus Christ was a soulwinner.

Before you were a teacher, you were a Christian. You have a call as a Christian to witness, to be a soulwinner. After that, you may be gifted as a teacher to teach Christians.

Before you were gifted to preach or teach prophecy in the church, you were a Christian. As a Christian, your first call is to win souls and your second call is to prophesy.

First, a Christian — a soulwinner. Then, a pastor.

First, a Christian — a soulwinner. Then, a teacher.

First, a Christian — a soulwinner. Then, a musician, singer, prophecy teacher, or whatever your gift is.

Always first, a Christian — a soulwinner.

Three Witnesses
Soulwinning first.

This is a principle in the kingdom of God.

I will share with you **three proofs — three witnesses — of this fact** from Luke 15:1-10.

Witness No. 1: *There is more joy in heaven over one sinner that repents than over ninety-nine persons who need no repentance* (v. 7).

Heaven rejoices when someone lost is found. One person who is won is a greater delight than 99 saved people.

In the kingdom of God, the priority is on the one who is lost.

Witness No. 2: In the kingdom of heaven, the Good Shepherd is pictured *leaving the ninety-nine* in the fold and going *out into the mountains,* **out to the dangerous places**, **out in the world**, to seek out the lost sheep (v. 4).

The Good Shepherd is not represented as staying in the fold, caring for the flock, but as going out after the lost one. He does that **through us** today.

As I said, this is a principle in the kingdom of God: Soulwinning — seeking out the lost person — first!

Witness No. 3: The good woman of the house is not pictured by the Master as sitting in her chair, counting and carefully polishing her treasured coins. But rather, she is occupied day and night, seeking *diligently till she finds* the lost coin (v. 8).

She lights her candle and searches patiently in the dark corners until she finds the lost coin, then she rejoices.

If the lost coin represents the unconverted, the scene is very different today. Sunday morning, the pastor polishes the "coins" which are safe in the fold — the church members.

During the week, they are polished again. The lost "coins" are never sought after.

Sunday after Sunday, there is more polishing of the "coins" which are already in the fold. Week after week, more ministry is directed to the already saved ones.

A teacher arrives who is gifted to expound the Word of God to Christians. Then the polishing is repeated every night during the series of meetings. Still there is no ministry to the **non-Christians**.

Then a prophecy teacher arrives. Still no attention is given to the **unconverted**.

Someone holds a series of special meetings to teach on the spiritual gifts, or on the types and shadows of the Old Testament. Still there is no outreach to **non-Christians**.

Singers entertain the Christians, followed by more "polishing." The *lost coin* is still not sought. The *lost sheep* are still not gone after.

Constant attention is given to those safe in the fold. Meanwhile, the **unconverted** continue to be **untouched** by Christians, **unreached** by soulwinners. **Christ cannot reach them because Christians do not go out after them.**

They will only see Christ and His love through us. He yearns to save them, but **He can only do it through us**.

God never called anyone to any ministry that was not a soulwinning ministry. **The very essence of being a Christian is to have Christ living in you — witnessing and ministering through you.**

The early church lived with a passion for souls. They were Christlike.

Whatever your talent in the church, you are first of all a soulwinner — first of all, a witness — **then** a writer, teacher, pastor, prophet, or whatever God has specifically gifted you for.

You can be a soulwinner — a real CHRIST-i-an! **Because Jesus was!**

T. L. and Daisy Osborn know the harvest is ripe and the laborers are few. They believe this book is an inspiration to thousands of Christians, worldwide to "thrust in their sickle and reap" (Rev. 14:15).

Osborn Crusade — Nigeria

5
Out Where The People Are

We are soulwinners because the harvest is so great.

No one can look into the faces of the masses bewildered by superstitious religions, as we have done, without doing their utmost to win souls.

For over three decades, we have stood on crude platforms out in the open air, before multitudes of underprivileged people, interspersed with lepers, demoniacs, witch doctors, and the hopelessly diseased. We have preached Christ to them when it was all one could do to hold back tears of human emotions.

Worldwide, there are millions who have not yet been reached. They constitute the vast, ripened harvest of souls waiting to be reaped.

This is the second reason why we are soulwinners: Because the harvest is so great.

The Bible says: *When Jesus saw the multitudes, he was moved with compassion on them, because they fainted, and were scattered abroad, as sheep having no shepherd* (Matt. 9:36).

Pondering these needy multitudes, He said, *The harvest truly is plenteous* (v. 37).

What did He do about it? He called twelve disciples, gave them power to cast out devils and heal the sick, and sent them out to help reap this harvest. Later, He called seventy more. Then before His ascension, He conferred upon all believers the power to witness with miracles in His name.

The fact is this: **He did something about this ripened harvest.** He did not just sit and ponder it and pray about it. He set about getting laborers out into these harvest fields.

Since Christ was *moved with compassion* when He saw the multitude and since we are like Christ, we also can be MOVED with compassion for or toward those who are untouched by the gospel. If we are, then, like Christ, we become involved doing something about sharing the gospel with them.

A pastor or Christian may say, "Oh, yes, we have compassion for the lost. We hold special prayer meetings each week, interceding for sinners to be saved. We are praying faithfully that people will be drawn into our church and be converted. We are having extra meetings and a special speaker to preach to the unconverted."

Did Christ tell us to go to church and ring a bell, to engage a special speaker and pray for sinners to come to our church to be saved?

Or did He say, *Go out into the highways and hedges, and compel them to come in, so that my house may be filled* (Luke 14:23)?

When we think of soulwinning, there is a principle to remember: Non-Christians do not go to church. We cannot reach them inside the church. To communicate the gospel to them, we must go **outside the church — out where they live, work and play.**

Certainly, a few can be reached in church meetings. But the rank and file of the unconverted multitudes will never go to church. They will never be contacted **inside** the church sanctuary. They may never meet Christ or know His love unless they see Him or hear of Him **through us** — witnessing and sharing Him **out where the people are**.

This truth cannot be over emphasized: **We** are Christ's body; He can only reach people **through us**.

The church must **go to them**. That is what Christ told His followers to do. That is what the early church believers did. In busy marketplaces, on street corners, at village wells, by the seaside, in the homes — these early Christians occupied themselves witnessing and winning souls.

Principle Of Evangelism

It was never God's plan that evangelism or soulwinning be carried on **inside** the church building. **Evangelism can only be effective out where the people are.**

The church building is the place where God's people come together to be nourished in the words of faith, taught in the doctrines of Christ, strengthened as Christians, and taught how to witness.

Soulwinning is done **out where the people live, work and play**.

The early church stayed busy *daily in*

the temple and in every house; they never stopped preaching and teaching Jesus Christ (Acts 5:42).

It is vital that we re-emphasize this basic principle in soulwinning.

We do not go fishing in our bathtubs. If we expect to catch fish, we cast our net away from our house, out in the streams, lakes, and waterways of the wilderness — **out where the fish are**.

We never harvest a crop inside our dining room. To reap the ripened grain, we wield our sickle through the heat of the day, away from the house, out in the broad fields — **out where the grain stands ripe and ready to be harvested.**

We do not win souls by staying **inside** our church building. To reap the unconverted, we carry our witness away from our sanctuaries, out into the markets, onto the streets, in jails, hospitals, houses of prostitution, in the homes of people, out among them — **out where they live, work and play. This is evangelism.**

We have dedicated over three decades of our lives to reaching people out where they are. This is why we build our platforms out in parks, on race tracks or stadium grounds, or out on fields.

Hindus do not go into a church.

Moslems do not enter a Christian temple.

Shintoists and Buddhists do not attend Christian worship.

The UNchurched do not come to church.

But when we **go out** with the gospel to public places — to seasides, parks, stadiums, race tracks or open fields, the unconverted come by the tens of thousands — Moslems, Hindus, Buddhists, NON-Christians. **We are out where they live and work and play.**

After we have won them **out where they are** and they have been converted, then they will come into the House of God to learn more of His Word and of the Christian faith.

The method of the early church was to go **out where the people are**.

This is where Peter and John shared their testimony when the crippled man was healed — **out on the streets**.

This is where Peter's great mass meetings were held in Jerusalem — **out in**

the streets and busy roadways.

This is where Philip preached to all of Samaria — **out in the public.** This is where he found the eunuch and led him to Christ — **out on the trader's roadway**.

This is where Paul convinced the heathen — **out on the island, among their people**.

A Farmer Reaps Out In The Field

Being raised on a farm as one of thirteen children I know what a ripened harvest looks like. I know the urgency of the harvest. When the broad fields of grain became ripe, we toiled relentlessly from early until late, reaping the harvest — **out where it grew**.

Then we would go to the house where a wonderful meal was prepared to nourish our weary bodies. After we had eaten, we went back to the fields to continue reaping until nightfall.

We toiled day after day, until the furthest corners of the vast fields were harvested.

Too often Christians are not taught to do this. If a program of soulwinning evangelism is attempted, it usually consists of special prayer meetings for people to be drawn into the church to be converted. Then a visiting teacher addresses the spiritual needs of the unconverted for a few nights. **But if they are not there, how can they be helped?**

This idea is alright, for the few who may attend and for those who have been won this way.

However, **we cannot think of reaching the world this way.** The ripened masses of the unconverted cannot be harvested **inside our churches** because the vast majority of them **will never come to our churches.**

If we really want to reap the harvest of our generation, the secret is to rediscover the passion and zeal of the early church. Those early Christians **went out** across cities and villages in constant pursuit of lost souls — even at the risk of their lives. **This is Christianity in action, being Christlike.**

As children on the farm, suppose we had eaten to our fill. Then, with our bodies strengthened and nourished, suppose we had looked out the window and pondered the ripened grain. Suppose ominous storm clouds were gathering, and the rumble of thunder was increasing.

What if we had knelt for a long afternoon of prayer, asking God to reap the harvest and to save the grain?

Suppose we had earnestly prayed: "Oh, God, save this grain; just send it our way so that we can reap it right here in our dining room."

Would not that sound strange?

Yet this is what many congregations have done. Too often they are not outside the church reaping the soul harvest of this generation.

Instead, they pray. "Oh, God, save lost souls; just draw them in to our lovely church so that we can get them saved right here."

It seems as though they are saying:

"Lord, how can we risk our reputation among unsaintly people.

"We dare not be seen witnessing to prostitutes, homosexuals, narcotic or alcohol dependants — out there in hell's half-acre where our reputation and the honor of our members might be at stake.

"You have given us this holy sanctuary where our reputation is protected. If You will just send the unconverted to us, we will pray for them in our sanctified environment and help them to be clean like we are."

Convenience Or Compassion

We have our lovely churches, our beautiful choirs, our comfortable pews. We are well equipped.

Is it fair to expect the unconverted to have to come to us to be saved? Would we not reach more of them by going out where they are?

Many Christians pray for the salvation of the unconverted, but never do anything about going out with Christ's love and giving them His message, out where they are. Yet, they call this compassion for the lost.

For hundreds of years, this philosophy has proven ineffective. I wonder if people cling to such ideas because they have not been taught otherwise?

In the early church, every believer was a witness, a soulwinner. Today, thousands of church members have never been encouraged to lead a soul to Christ

— the idea never occured to them.

Most of them would not know the first step to take in actually leading an unbeliever to Christ on the spot.

The early church method — God's idea — was for every believer to be a witness, a soulwinner then to go out in the highways and hedges and compel people to come in, *so that His house may be filled.*

We are to win people **out where they are.** Then they will come to the House of God to be nourished in faith by the pastor and by teachers. Why? For one reason: So they may return to the ripened fields to join the reapers in saving the lost.

What A Church Can Do

I recommend to you — whether you are a pastor, a teacher, or a church worker — that you determine not only to learn to win souls yourself, but to share with and inspire other Christians around you to do the same.

New steps can be taken at once to plant ideas among those under your influence. Think of every possible idea to motivate Christian friends and acquaintances to go **out where people are to share Christ**.

Get extra copies of this book, and of its sequel, or companion book, *Join This Chariot*. Then make an investment in the lives of other Christians by giving them copies to inspire them. You can motivate people to success, happiness and greater self-esteem by encouraging them to reach out and lift others this way.

Many years ago we decided to **do something** to encourage Christians worldwide.

To inspire this kind of Christian witnessing, out where the people live, work and play, **we sent over 100,000 gift copies** of this and its companion book on soulwinning, to special ministers, pastors, evangelists, missionaries, and national church leaders around the world as an investment in the ministry of believers everywhere.

Now as we observe the effect of that investment, we can see that those two books have proven to be the SEEDS from which a revival of **Soulwinning - Out**

Where The People Are has literally spread throughout the free world.

There are so many workable, effective ideas for reaching people and for sharing Christ with them. Buy two or three small tents or rent some halls, shops or rooms; then invite a few Christian friends to operate in each location of your area. Equip them with literature and other tools — videos, films, tapes and literature.

Invest in ten portable audio or video cassette players. Invite ten qualified Christians to take a machine, equipped with recorded sermons, music, and good gospel literature and witness out in the streets, homes, play areas, bars, beaches and businesses, of ten different sections of your town.

The Ten Towns

As soon as Jesus cast the demons out of the naked demoniac, and he believed on Christ, they clothed him and Jesus sent him out to witness to the **ten towns** called the Decapolis. (See Mark 5:19-20 L.B.) *The man began to tell everyone about the great things Jesus had done for* *him*. He was just a new convert, but what a powerful witness he was for Christ.

The Lord may have **ten** supermarkets for you to reach, or **ten** convalescent homes, **ten** blocks, **ten** counties, **ten** villages, **ten** communities or **ten** houses. For Daisy and me, it has been nearly **70 nations**.

So — get **your** idea. Dream **your** dream. Stock up, then **go for it**.

Stamp your church name on each tract or book and encourage each worker to go out where the people are to win them. Inspire them to witness, to pray for the sick, and to lead souls to Christ on the spot.

During the day, they can canvass each area, leading many to Christ right in their own homes.

At night, they can preach or teach or use their audio or video cassettes or films and win souls in their public meetings.

On Sundays, these Christian workers can bring their newly won families into their own church. There the pastor can nourish them in God's Word and train them until they, too, become soulwinners in their areas.

Some Christians will want to go to jails, others to hospitals (with headsets on their cassette players so they will not disturb other patients), others to convalescent homes and other special areas.

Youth groups, supplied with cassettes, books, tracts, and musical instruments, can witness on street corners, in residential areas, in shopping centers, in market places — wherever there are people, **out where they live, work and play**.

Christ can only show His love to people through Christians. Remember that each believer is Christ's body today and that He can only reach the lost **through believers.**

A whole new vision will soon grip your Christian friends. They will gain a fresh passion for souls, a zeal for soul-winning.

Paint a large banner and hang it inside your church or classroom where everyone can see it:

Our Motto: Every Christian, A Witness!

Our Mission: Out Where the People Are!

Banners are effective. When we attended Dr. Oswald J. Smith's evangelism convention many years ago, the very atmosphere was alive with banners. Just sitting and reading them inspired us.

It is an old technique, but it always works. Did you ever notice how demonstrators carry banners in their parades?

All week long, engage in a busy program of soulwinning. On Sundays and some mid-week evenings, let the soulwinners gather at the House of God to be nourished and inspired by His Word. But then let them return in their new strength to harvest again, **out where the people are**.

This is the vision of the happy believer.

This gives excitement to Christian living.

This makes Christian living truly objective.

This eliminates depression and loneliness.

This adds enthusiasm to your church.

This is evangelism as it was practiced by the early church.

Mushrooming all around us, in every

city and country, is a generation unreached by the gospel — religious in many
ways, but unaware of the reality of Jesus
Christ.

This is the ripened harvest. Christ can
only reap that harvest **through us. We**
are His body today.

Daisy, my wife, and I have already
invested over three decades in reaping
this harvest. This is what has inspired us
to reach almost 70 nations already. Literally MILLIONS have believed on Christ.

This is the second reason we are soulwinners: **The harvest truly is great.**

"The preaching of the cross is to them who perish foolishness; but to (those who believe and) are saved, it is the power of God" (1 Cor. 1:18).

6
Here Am I

We are soulwinners because the laborers are so few!

Also I heard the voice of the Lord, saying Whom shall I send, and who will go for us? Then said I, Here am I; send me— (Is. 6:8).

World population is increasing at the rate of over seventy million per year. Do you know that less than three million of that increase is being touched by the gospel?

It is a fair estimate that there are perhaps two billion souls **who have never heard the gospel.**

This represents nearly half the world's population, including tribespeople who speak over 1,000 different languages.

A lost world is racing toward eternity at a terrifying speed.

In Japan, for example, after over four hundred years of gospel ministry, the overwhelming majority of the hundred million people are still non-Christian. Most of Japan's 95,000 rural communities have **no Christian witness**.

Yet there is a tremendous response to the gospel wherever the opportunity exists to hear it, especially among Japan's youth. Those engaged in literature, radio and TV evangelism receive over half of all responses from the 15-25 age group.

Young Japan is ripe for harvesting, but where are the laborers?

About one out of three people today live in China where the gospel has been so limited.

Almost two million people commit suicide annually.

Thirty times more souls are born than converts are made.

On an average, Moslems send 4,000 teachers south of the Sahara each year. They have been converting the Africans to Islam at a much faster rate than the Christians have been winning them to Christ.

Scientific materialism and atheism are everywhere, opposing the Christian message.

The golden opportunity for Christians is to reap this vast human harvest with renewed enthusiasm and dedication.

Looking On The Fields

Jesus said, *Lift up your eyes, and look on the fields; for they are white already to harvest* (John 4:35).

Again He said, *The harvest truly is plenteous, but the laborers are few; pray ye therefore the Lord of the harvest, that he will send forth laborers into his harvest* (Matt. 9:37,38).

We have looked and have seen the harvest fields. We have prayed for more laborers. But above all, we are giving our lives, reaping this harvest.

That is why we are soulwinners: Because the laborers are so few.

In India, there is a district of 77 villages where a recent census showed there was **not one Christian among them**. No national pastor, missionary or evangelist had ever preached the gospel there.

Those people live and die without Christ — not because they have rejected Him, but because during the last 2,000 years, not one Christian has gone to share with them the gospel of His love.

The harvest is ripe, but the laborers are few.

While 94% of all ministers of the gospel in the world are preaching in comparative comfort to the 9% English-speaking people, a lonely 6% of them are struggling to meet the spiritual needs of the remaining 91% of the world!

We have chosen to give the best of our lives to sharing Christ where the need is greatest and where the workers are fewest. That is why we have taken every possible step to multiply our lives by producing and providing tools for evangelism for the church of this century, around the world.

By recording our voices on magnetic tape, video cassettes and film (with the help of anointed national interpreters), we can reach hundreds of tribes simultaneously, regardless of the many different dialects they may speak.

When a national Christian — perhaps one who has not yet been trained to preach well — switches on a good cassette unit, another proficient soulwinner is in the making.

After a few weeks, our message is absorbed by that worker and our manner of evangelism is learned. The unit can then be given to another untrained worker and the process is repeated. In the meantime another preacher is out proclaiming the same gospel messages. This is proving effective worldwide.

Each time a documentary crusade film is shown to crowds of thousands in the Philippines, in Thailand, in Africa, or in any other nation, this again is multiplying another soulwinning operation — and it works at home as well as abroad.

Every time a gospel tract is passed from hand to hand, the message of Life is being reproduced.

You too, can increase your gospel witness with literature, by sending more witnessing tools to the mission fields of this generation, and by putting more evangelism tools to work on the home front.

Why are we soulwinners? **Because the laborers are so few.**

"Why should anyone hear the Gospel twice before everyone has heard it once?" T. L. and Daisy have shared the Gospel with MILLIONS face to face, in 70 nations.

7
The Choice to Win

We are soulwinners because of the Great Commission.

The last thing Jesus authorized us to do before He went away was: *Go ye to all the world, and preach the gospel to every creature* (Mark 16:15).

This is His authority to each of His followers. This is the greatest opportunity He offered to us. This is every Christian's privilege, calling, purpose, and ministry.

When God's love overflowed to the point that He gave His only begotten Son, it was for *the whole world,* so that *whoever believes in him will not perish, but will have everlasting life* (John 3:16).

Christ left us no privilege greater than to announce the gospel to every creature. This is the believer's guarantee of happiness.

This is what the early Christians did day and night. They witnessed from house to house, at markets, village wells, on the busy roadways, on the streets, in meeting places, from jail cells, in dungeons, everywhere.

They understood their calling. They did as Christ did. They knew He was living in them, doing through them the same things He had done before He was crucified. That is why they were called CHRIST-i-ans.

Many churches do not encourage this concept. Most Christians are church members, but few are witnesses. They go to their sanctuaries, but not to the by-ways, to tell people of Christ.

There is a principle to be remembered: Non-Christians do not usually go to church.

Therefore, we can never reach them **inside** the church building. We must go **out** after them — **out where they are** — as Jesus authorized us to do. **He is in us. We are His body.** He can only reach people **through us**.

Perhaps no couple in this generation has followed such a basic pattern of evangelism for so long a time as Daisy, my wife, and I have. We have already dedicated over three decades of our lives giving the simple gospel of Christ to people **out in public places.**

If you had walked on the grounds of

our earliest campaigns, then attended a recent crusade, you would have heard the same gospel, presented with the same simplicity. You would observe the same strategy, heard the same prayers, seen the same miracles.

The Great Commission of Christ is the reason behind this ministry and its entire design. Our motto is **One Way; One Job.**

The **One Way** is Jesus.

The **One Job** is evangelism.

Every phase of each operation is aimed at reaching the unconverted — the unchurched — with the gospel, **reaching them out where they are.**

As Christians, that has been our choice. Christ lives in us. **We are His body.** We want Him to win souls **through us**.

Only One Purpose

We live and breathe for **one purpose: to share the gospel with the maximum number of people, by every means possible.** We use not only our own voices as Christ speaks through us, but also channels of mass media, reproduction, duplication, and every form of dissemination we can utilize.

Our world ministry, as it is known today, was not planned by us. No such design entered our minds at its beginning.

What happened?

We simply chose to obey Christ's Great Commission. We accepted it as our life's work. We chose to invest ourselves completely, sharing the gospel with every person we could reach.

We have conducted almost a steady stream of public gospel crusades, preaching face to face to literally millions.

But this was not enough. These meetings only lasted two or three hours each day. What about the other hours of those days?

It dawned on us that we could write the same message that we preached. Giant presses could turn them out by the millions — by the tons — in every written language on earth. This way we could reach hundreds of millions of extra souls who would never hear the sound of our voices.

For years, we averaged publishing

over a ton of gospel tracts every working day — not counting the additional tons of our books and magazines pouring monthly into the nations of the world. This literature has been rolling off the world's presses in 132 different languages.

With the world's masses becoming literate at the rate of three million per week (over 150 million per year) and with their insatiable thirst for reading material, the printing of faith literature opens the door for us to reach every **literate** person with the gospel message.

In addition to our crusades and literature ministries, we still could do more. What about the **illiterate** millions? Most of the underprivileged masses cannot read or write.

To reach these, we have utilized the remarkable sound devices of this century — the audio and the video tape, and the motion film. What fantastic possibilities exist here for both personal evangelism, as well as TV and radio outreaches to the unchurched.

So we began to preach on film and on tape the same good news that we had proclaimed to millions in our audiences, and to create tools for soulwinners as well as for mass media release.

Soon the wheels of two additional outreaches were rolling. Our sound production team began duplicating those anointed crusade sermons in sight and sound in scores of languages, with more being added at every opportunity.

Today, tens of thousands of audio and video cassettes as well as documentary crusade films, in over 60 languages, are operating in the hands of national church leaders, evangelists, pastors, and gospel ministers in nations worldwide and on the Christian home fronts, attracting more millions to the gospel.

One pastor alone showed one of our films twenty times in one province. He reached 50,000 souls and witnessed more than 8,000 decisions for Christ.

Another minister reported 2,000 decisions in only eight days of film ministry. These figures are multiplied into almost infinity as these tools are released via mass media.

Jesus said, *Preach the gospel to every*

creature. We pondered the millions of tribespeople living far beyond the fringes of civilization, out of the range of missionaries or national church leaders, without the luxury of TV or radio. These also must hear the gospel. There are over 2,000 tribes like this who do not comprehend the languages used for mass media. We prayed for ways to help reach them too.

To this end, our national evangelism world outreach program was born. God showed us how we could inspire Christians in the more prosperous nations of the world to share a certain amount of money each month to personally sponsor a national preacher as a missionary to those tribes.

We alerted soulwinning missions around the world with this vision. As they began to recruit qualified national Christians who would risk their lives to go to the interior of those neglected areas, we began to recruit Christian sponsors. The delicate balance of demand and supply has been a constant miracle since this program of national evangelism was inaugurated.

Many thousands of national missionaries have been sponsored in over a hundred nations, reaching innumberable unreached tribes and areas with the gospel.

An average of over one new church per day has been opened and has become self-supporting. That is almost 400 new churches per year, for many years. Never in church history had such a far-reaching evangelism effort been effected.

God Increased Our Best

As a lad with a toy press, printing scripture verses on scraps of paper, I did my best.

And God increased our best.

Each year greater ideas and greater capacities developed as we kept reaching out for better methods and concepts to win more souls.

We are doing our utmost to share the gospel. We constantly apply every talent possible and grasp every available opportunity and method to evangelize. Because of this, there has developed this enormous ministry of world evangelism with its globe-circling influence.

It has been like planting good seeds. They always grow, and harvests continue to increase.

Our persistent goal has been to reach non-Christians — the unchurched, the unevangelized — not the already Christian populace.

Many ask, "Why don't you conduct your campaigns in churches?"

Simply because non-Christians do not go to church. **To reach them, we go to them. We go out where they are.**

Jesus said, *Preach to every creature.*

If one nation is 95% Christian while another is 95% non-Christian, our choice is to reach the non-Christian nation.

If a small field of ripened grain had a hundred reapers at work in it, while a large field had only one reaper, which field would you toil in to save the grain? You would choose the field where the need is greatest and where there are the fewest to meet the need.

If ten people were lifting a log — nine on the small end and one on the large end — it would not be difficult to choose where you would lift.

Opportunities Worldwide

You do not need a special call to be a soulwinner. Your golden opportunity as a Christian is to let your light shine, to witness, to share the gospel with the unchurched. **This is your finest purpose in life.**

This is why it is objective for any professional to move to a gospel neglected nation and operate a business or a profession where it can facilitate a ministry of witnessing and soulwinning.

Whether you are a mechanic, pharmacist, artist, mason, dentist, photographer, plumber, carpenter, engineer or capable of any other profession or skill — re-situate yourself and your family in an unevangelized nation. Your profession will be desperately needed and heartily welcomed. While you practice your trade or profession or skill, you can carry out a constant ministry of witnessing to non-Christians. **You do not have to be an ordained minister to share the gospel. This is the privilege of every believer.**

These nations, tribes and areas can only learn of Christ and see His love and compassion, as Christians live and witness among them. Christ can never reach them without a body, and **we are His body**. He can only be seen **in us**. His good news can only be heard **through us**. **He can only speak through our lips.**

For too long, the great business opportunities overseas have been monopolized by unconverted people. Non-Christians with a zest for adventure, rush through these open doors. They establish their businesses or agencies abroad, then revel in a non-Christian lifestyle among the people.

Meanwhile, Christians of integrity and high moral standards remain at home, assuming that they must have a missionary call before they can go abroad and witness of Christ. They do not comprehend that **they are Christ's body**, that Christ can only reach these developing nations **through human beings in whom He lives.** They wait for **the church** to do the job, forgetting that **they are the church**.

Christian professionals are the ones who should take advantage of these business and professional opportunities overseas. Their careers will yield fruitful soulwinning ministries and will be instrumental in carrying out Christ's commission.

Christians do not need a special call to do things Christ authorized to be done throughout the world. They only need to see the world as God sees it and to accept the honor of being one of His ambassadors of righteousness.

Our Master asks, *Whom shall I send, and who will go for us?*

You can answer with Isaiah: *Here am I, Lord. Send me.*

Go and share the gospel with as many people as you can reach. The call has been given. The opportunities are plentiful. The need is urgent. Success is assured. You, as Christ's ambassador, are authorized to be involved. You need no further calling.

As you begin to think about your world and inform yourself about conditions in various areas of the globe, you will be guided by God's Spirit within you, to where the opportunity is greatest and the need for Christian messengers is the most urgent.

Paul was enroute to Asia on a certain occasion, but was *forbidden of the Holy Ghost. Then he tried going into Bithynia: but the Spirit suffered them not ... then a vision appeared to Paul in the night.* In this vision, *a man of Macedonia prayed him, saying, Come over into Macedonia, and help us* (Acts 16:6-9).

That is the kind of guidance you may receive, if you stay sensitive and alert in your spirit. Paul was already an apostle, an evangelist, going throughout his world, preaching the gospel. As he was going to yet other *regions beyond,* he received this guidance to Macedonia.

This has happened to us numerous times. Once we were determined to go to India. As we were on our way, we were impressed of the Lord to change our course to the southern tip of the Philippines. Our obedience resulted in a glorious mass crusade among those needy people.

Often we are guided this way. Usually it happens when we are in action. Our constant understanding with our Father is this:

"Lord, if there is any certain field or area or nation where You want us, show us and we will go. But if You do not, we will choose the best opportunity to reap the most fruitful harvest and we will be there reaping until You guide us elsewhere."

Jesus said, *Lo, I am with you alway* (Matt. 28:20). He is in us. We are His body. We go so that He can reach the people. He speaks and witnesses and ministers **through us**. He is concerned for the whole world.

Our orders are given: *Go to ALL the world. Preach to EVERY creature.*

This is our mission. Christ's words are to be acted upon — not analyzed, argued, or theorized.

Our Open Doors

The unconverted world is hurting. They have problems without answers, diseases without remedies, fears without faith, guilt without pardon.

Christ's last words to His followers was his authorization to go help, heal, lift and love them — and to win them. They afford us our golden opportunity and they guarantee our success, self-esteem and total happiness in life.

As we lift them, we are lifted. Healing them, we are healed. Loving them, we are loved. In serving them, we are truly serving our Lord.

When we stand before Him, He will commend us: *I was hungry and you gave me meat. I was thirsty and you gave me to drink. I was a stranger and you took me in; Naked and you clothed me. I was sick and you visited me. I was in prison and you came to me ... Inasmuch as you did it unto one of the least of these ... you did it unto me* (Matt. 25:35-40).

These are our open doors!

Jesus Christ died for the whole world. His blood was shed for the remission of the sins of every person on earth who will call upon Him (Matt. 26:28).

But, *how can they call on him if they have not believed? And how can they believe on him if they have not heard? ... So then faith* (to be saved) *comes by hearing ... the word of God* (Rom. 10:14,17).

You and I are the witnesses, the confessors, the testifiers, the voices, the preachers, the instruments through which this world can *hear* the gospel. Christ lives and ministers through us.

This is the last thing Jesus authorized us to do. It constitutes our finest and most productive lifestyle.

Daisy and I have chosen to share Christ with people. **We are soulwinners because of the Great Commission of Jesus Christ.**

8
The Forgotten Ones

We are soulwinners because of the unfulfilled prophecies concerning Jesus' return.

It has almost become a tradition for teachers to emphasize the soon return of Christ by declaring, "Every prophecy has been fulfilled which precedes His second coming."

But is this true? Perhaps the most important sign of all has not been fulfilled. That sign concerns you and me. It involves us as Christians and our ministry as witnesses.

Jesus specified several *signs of His coming;* among them false christs, wars, nations in conflict, famines, pestilences, earthquakes, persecutions, deceit, lack of consecration. (See Matt. 24:4-12.)

Then He added, *And this gospel of the kingdom shall be preached in all the world for a witness unto all nations; and then shall the end come* (Matt. 24:14).

Christ's last words, before He returned to the Father, were — in essence: *Go now to all nations and proclaim to*

*every creature the good news. As soon as
you do this, I shall return.* Has this been
done yet?

I can imagine impetuous Peter nudg-
ing John and saying, "Come on, John.
Let's hurry. This won't take long. Then
He'll come back to us."

The early church understood their
mission. Not only the apostles, but **each
believer was a witness**.

Day by day — in houses, on streets,
at village wells and markets, on roadways
— they preached Christ and won souls.
Their objective was to reach *every creature* and *all nations* as rapidly as possible
— in spite of deadly opposition —
because as soon as they finished, Jesus
Christ would return.

They knew that Christ was not dead,
but lived in them, doing the same things
He did before He was crucified. They
understood that Christ could only speak
and witness through them.

This concept of soulwinning so motivated the early Christians that they spread
the gospel testimony across most of their
known world.

Down across the Mediterranean, the

message went until one time North Africa was dotted with Christian places of worship. Braving storms, dangers at sea, perils of ancient travel, and every conceivable hardship, they spread the message with unequalled gallantry.

Then instead of charting camel caravans south of the Sahara into the African jungles, or pressing eastward beyond the continental mountain barriers, or northward to the pagan tribes, they became more interested in conserving what they had. **They failed to press on to the uttermost parts.**

Conventions began to replace evangelism. Doctrinal disputes superseded personal witnessing. Soon the church began to lose power and sank into the Dark Ages.

The decline came when Christians lost the basic concept of *Christ in you*. They no longer considered themselves individually as Christ's body and as His voice. They created religious organizations, calling those entities "the church." Darkness prevailed and Christ was not shared with unbelievers.

It was hundreds of years later when

Martin Luther perceived that *the just shall live by faith* (Heb. 10:38) and the reformation began. The church began her slow rediscovery of early church evangelism.

The Wesleys, preaching **sanctification**, followed by the 20th century revival of **the baptism of the Holy Spirit** were further steps in the slow revival of effective Christianity.

From God's viewpoint, these truths were unveiled afresh so that Christians might be empowered to witness in *all the world,* among *all nations,* to *every creature* — and thus bring back the King.

They Left The Forgotten Ones

But the church did not hold God's viewpoint. Tradition concerning Christ's return blinded them to the purpose of Pentecost.

Rather than witnessing with power to the unsaved in houses, on streets, in markets — **out where the people are** — they segregated themselves with innumerable sectarian barriers and denominational labels.

They left **the forgotten ones** to their own pitiful fate while they withdrew into religious communities and councils. They ignored the cry of the unreached, defending their doctrines, proselyting members and placating themselves with their own religious ceremonies.

As a whole, church members have not skilled themselves in going **out where the unconverted world lives**.

We can never witness to the world — to the masses of unchurched multitudes — **from within our sanctuaries**. Non-Christians do not go to church.

The church was commissioned to go to the people: *Go out quickly into the streets and lanes of the city. Go out into the highways and hedges. Go into all the world. Go to every creature.*

Jesus told us to **go out where the people are** and to win them exactly as He did — not in religious sanctuaries, **but out where they live, work and play.**

Has this been done? Has this gospel been preached *as a witness unto all nations* as Christ said shall be done prior to His return?

Over one half of our generation is unreached by the gospel. They have never heard the good news even once. They are **the forgotten ones** of our time.

Why should anyone hear the gospel twice before everyone has heard it once?

Over a thousand tribes have never had a gospel witness. Reaching these people is, therefore, the sign which Christ foretold, but which has not yet been fulfilled.

This is the sign which concerns you and me. We are authorized to reach the unreached with the gospel of Christ.

This is why we are doing everything we can to win souls and to encourage every other Christian to be a soulwinner.

This is why we have developed a whole arsenal of tools for evangelism. With these, we equip soulwinners around the world to increase their soul harvest as they go out in search of these forgotten ones.

These were Christ's last words to us.

This was the only thing He left us to do.

Has the church accomplished this yet?

Learn From Revolutionaries

What an object lesson political revolutionaries are for Christians. Did you ever think of it?

They invade and infiltrate developing nations. Their leaders retreat to the hills, the jungles, the swamps, and from there impose controls on local tribes.

Once entrenched among these forgotten people where disease and poverty are rampant, they organize guerilla bands and begin their hit and run harassment. First, villages; then towns and cities; their aim is always a national takeover.

These political and mercenary leaders go to the very people which the church has often neglected. They pay any price and make any sacrifice to live in the most difficult areas.

The modern gospel messenger has not been equipped or encouraged to reach these people. In general, they would scarcely survive in such areas, so these tribes have been left without Christ. Whereas, the insurgents send in their teachers to live completely indigenous and make the utmost sacrifice — life itself, to organize these tribes into forces for their purpose.

What the church has not done, revolutionaries have done. The very people who have been neglected by the church, have become a hotbed for enemy seed sowing.

What an example they are to the Christian church. Insurrectionists go where the church has not gone and mobilize the people for their harassment teams and take over nations.

Yet Christian teachers take the position: "All signs are fulfilled. Come quickly, Lord Jesus."

Can this be the attitude of a Christian?

Our privilege as Christians has not been withdrawn since Christ gave His commission. First, we are to give the gospel to every nation; **then** the end shall come.

This is why Daisy and I are soulwinners, **because this prophecy is still unfulfilled.**

It concerns us — and it concerns you. Christ died for *every creature.* **But He can only reach them through us. We are His body today.**

This is why most of our public ministry has been **among the unchurched masses** of nations abroad. These are the unreached. They do not come to a church. **We go out after them — out where they are**, so that Christ can speak to them **through us**. We reach them to the limit of our possibilities.

Naturally it would be more convenient and we would prefer living our lives surrounded with the comforts of home. However, our opportunity as Christians is to witness to the maximum number of souls by every available means.

This is what we have done and what we continue doing.

Our Unfinished Task

Jesus said in Mark 13:10, *The gospel must first be published among all nations.*

There are over 3,000 languages spoken and over a third of them do not yet have a single gospel portion published in them.

Has the church done what Christ said must first be done?

This is why for many years we have published faith books and salvation tracts by the tons, in over 100 languages. We choose to do our utmost to reach **these forgotten ones**. As long as our evangelism partners share with us, we shall continue publishing the gospel in more and more dialects.

Sometimes it is argued that: "Every *nation* has had the gospel at one time or another."

Evidently our Lord knew such voices would be raised. In The Revelation, He showed the Apostle John things to come. John's words are vital for the soulwinner. He writes:

After this I beheld, and, lo, a great multitude, which no man could number, of all nations, and kindreds, and people, and tongues, stood before the throne, and before the Lamb, clothed with white robes, and palms in their hand;

And cried with a loud voice, saying, Salvation to our God which sits upon the throne, and unto the Lamb (Rev. 7:9-10).

This is the multitude of the redeemed, gathered to worship before God's throne.

And it will be as John saw it.

And how can they hear Christ's gospel if He cannot speak **through us?**

We are His body today — His lips, His voice. We are to go and let Christ speak **through us** to them. This is the

Among this multitude were those from *all nations*. It mentions *nations* first.

Some say, "I'm sure that all *nations* have heard the gospel."

Yes, perhaps, but the vision was more specific than that. The Holy Spirit went on to detail all *kindreds, and people and tongues*.

If Christ returned today, this scene could not be as John saw it. To be included in that multitude, they must hear the gospel, believe it, and be redeemed through the blood of the Lamb.

John said, *I saw another angel fly in the midst of heaven, having the everlasting gospel to preach unto them that dwell on the earth, and to every nation, and kindred, and tongue, and people* (Rev. 14:6).

But, Paul asks, *how shall they believe in him of whom they have not heard?* (Rom. 10:14).

way they can hear and believe.

Over a thousand *peoples* have not heard the gospel, not even once. Christ has not been able to reach them because Christians have not gone to them; and He will not send angels to do what He wills to do **through us**.

Over a third of the *tongues* of the world have not yet had the gospel published in them. If Christ came today, could those hundreds of *kindreds* be there to cry, *Salvation to our God, and unto the Lamb.*

This prophecy is not fulfilled yet.

God's No. 1 Job

This is why we have sponsored so many thousands of national sons and daughters of the soil — national gospel ministers who have been enabled, with our assistance, **to go and live among these unreached areas and tribes and to preach the gospel to them.**

This is soulwinning. This is evangelism — what Christ authorized us to do. This is ministering life **among the forgotten ones**.

We talk of Christ's Second Coming,

while millions have never heard of His first coming.

We insist on second blessings, while these **forgotten ones** have never tasted of a first blessing.

We argue about a refilling, while multitudes have never experienced a first filling.

Is this fair? Should those on the front row receive a second serving before the hungry ones on the back rows have received a first serving?

We have dedicated this ministry to the back rows, to the unchurched, to the unsaved, to these forgotten ones. Is not this the Christian's greatest mission in life? Is this not a guarantee of success, happiness and fulfillment?

Once these forgotten ones are remembered as they should be, those prophecies will be fulfilled and Jesus will return for His church. That is why we are soulwinners — to bring back the King.

T. L. Osborn addresses international convention in the United States.

9

Top Priority

We are soulwinners because we do not want the blood of the unconverted on our hands!

As a young Christian, one of the Bible portions which impressed me was Ezekiel 3:17-20.

God specifically speaks to His servants about the purpose of sharing His message with people so they can be blessed.

I have made you a watcher ... give warning from me.

When I say to the wicked, you shall surely die; and you give no warning ... to save lives; the wicked shall die in their iniquity;

But their blood will I require at your hand.

Again in Ezekiel 33:6, God repeats this message:

If the watcher sees the sword come, and blows not the trumpet, and the people are not warned; if the sword comes and takes any person from among them, they are taken away in their iniquity;

But their blood will I require at the watcher's hand.

Then in Ezekiel 33:8, the same idea is re-emphasized.

Here are three witnesses to let us know that we can do something about the unconverted that will cause them to be saved instead of being lost.

I am a great believer in applying scriptures in a personal, practical way. Let's read one of these verses made applicable to the soulwinner today:

I have made you a watcher. Therefore, hear the word at My mouth and give warning from Me.

When I say to sinners, You shall surely die, and you give to them no warning, nor speak to warn them of their sinful ways, to save their lives; the same sinners will die in their iniquities. But their blood will I require at your hand!

Yet if you warn sinners and they turn not from their sinfulness, nor from their sinful ways, they shall die in their iniquities. But you have delivered your soul.

This Motivated My Life

Their blood will I require at your hand.

Each time we read these words, we review our priorities. That scripture has motivated us since we were teenagers. **We do not want the blood of the unconverted required at our hands.**

This is another reason we are soulwinners.

This is why we share the gospel.

This is why Daisy and I have given, and continue to give, our lives to world-wide gospel crusades — why we have consistently done everything we can, using every tool for evangelism available to reach the unreached.

This is why we have led this ministry in sponsoring many thousands of national preachers as gospel messengers among the unchurched masses.

This is why we publish hundreds of tons of gospel literature in 132 languages and dialects.

This is why we produce films and audio or video tapes in over sixty major languages as tools for soulwinners and for release through mass media.

This is why we have witnessed the enormous growth of this world ministry. We simply share the gospel.

This is why we stay on the go.

This is the reason for every outreach of this ministry, and why we encourage faithful Christians to be partners with us. By sharing in these outreaches, our partners become soulwinners with us among these **forgotten ones** and share the rewards just as much as those who go to the front lines.

We are people who have received word from the Lord. We give warning *to flee from the wrath to come* (Matt. 3:7).

In the words of the Apostle Paul: *Woe unto me if I do not preach the gospel* (1 Cor. 9:16). We do not want the blood of the unconverted on our hands — either at home or abroad. **So we choose to be soulwinners.**

It's Up To Us

We do not pretend that we alone can win the world to Christ; **but we are involved in evangelism as though God's plan depended on us alone.**

If we cannot win everyone, we shall certainly win some — **and we shall minister as though the reaping depended entirely upon us**.

A sophisticated businesswoman of prominence, who was touring our world headquarters in Tulsa, Oklahoma, requested to see me and was, therefore, welcomed into our offices.

She was inquisitive and intelligent. I responded to her probings; then she gave me a final sizing up with these words: "Dr. Osborn, you seem to be very wrapped up in what you call world evangelism. Do you think your activities alone will win the whole world to Christ?"

Responding to her question, I replied, **"No, but we intend to be involved as though the entire opportunity was entrusted to us."**

She was pleased and became a partner with us in soulwinning.

We are soulwinners because we have taken God's word seriously. We do not want the blood of the unconverted to ever be required at our hands. It is as simple as that!

In my estimation, **the most important opportunity in the life of any
Christian** — not just ministers, but all
Christians — **is to witness to the unconverted.** Christ only reaches them
**through men and women in whom He
lives.**

Soulwinning is not a pastime or a
hobby. **Soulwinning is Christianity in
action every day.**

As soon as we are saved, we can
share Christ with others. We are Christ's
voice, His mouthpiece. If we are silent,
Christ is silenced. **He only speaks
through us.**

This is not something we do when it
is convenient. **Soulwinning is our number one priority in life — our life's
greatest opportunity!**

Wouldn't it be wonderful if soulwinning became the major theme of every
Bible school, every youth group, every
Sunday School, every Bible conference
and convention?

Christians are successful in every
conceivable art, trade or profession. They
can also be successful in soulwinning
because **this is the number one priority**

of every believer. More of them would succeed at this if more were taught that they, as individuals, are Christ's body and that **Christ only ministers and speaks through the body in which He dwells — the believer**.

Spread across the east stone wall of the lobby of our world headquarters in Tulsa is a beautiful map of the world. Positioned to the right and left of the map, in metal letters are the words:

One Way - Jesus
One Job - Evangelism

The attention of all visitors is focused on this motto to impress upon them the fact that this is a **trans-world** ministry. When God loved, He loved a world. When He gave His Son, He did it for a world. When Christ died, He died for a world.

God's vision is a world vision.

Our vision is like His.

Measure The Vision

Many people are localized in their vision. They see **their** community. They think of **their** church or denomination but have no interest beyond that.

Others have a broader vision, spreading out to their state or province or tribe. They are concerned with evangelizing that area, but do not feel responsible beyond those limits.

Still others see their whole country and will give and pray for the evangelization of their own nation. But even they are local in their vision. They are what we call **nationalistic** in their soulwinning interests.

There are others who have an even broader vision that reaches out to their continent. They are interested in **continental** evangelism and will make any sacrifice to reach their continent. But even they are localized.

Then there are those Christians who have **God's vision — a world vision, a John 3:16 vision**. They see Europe, Asia, Africa, North and South America, Australia, the Island nations — all the world, *every creature*. They have a **transworld** vision.

With jet aircraft, TV and satellite communication, we live on a small crowded planet. As Christians, our vision can be a world vision. Racial and political barriers are as foreign to God's plan as denominational and sectarian walls ever were.

Christians no longer ask what church one belongs to or what creed one ascribes to. They ask, "Do you know Jesus Christ, the Son of God, as your personal Savior and Lord?"

Many times we have boarded a plane, soared off the runway of some intercontinental airport, climbed to a great altitude, and looked down upon the vast countryside as we flew across nations, then continents, then oceans and islands, then more nations.

As I have looked down from such heights, I have pondered the soulwinners we had left behind who had been **localized** in their vision until we came. They had been limited by the attitudes, culture or religious philosophy of their denomination or club or society. They had not looked or reached beyond the borders of their city or area or nation. They had not traveled, or expanded their world by reading.

After our ministry, however, they had gotten God's viewpoint of their world.

Their vision was no longer localized. They had become concerned for the whole world. **As a result of our seminars, we know of Africans engaged in evangelism in China; South Americans going to win souls in Alaska; Indonesians reaching the lost in Europe; Asians ministering in the Caribbean.**

The light which God has imparted to us when He gave us Eternal Life can shine in dark places all across the world, as we share God's vision and understand the basic truth of Christianity — **that we are Christ's body today — vessels through which He reaches the world.**

Another vital phrase of our motto on the lobby wall of our world headquarters is **"Around the Clock - Around the World."**

Probe The Priorities

We show by our actions what we feel is most important. If trans-world soulwinning is our **priority**, then we give it first place.

This is why most of our crusades are conducted **overseas**, why most of our literature is published in languages for the

peoples afar, why most of our funds are used **abroad**, why most of our evangelism projects are geared for the **unreached**, why most of our films, tapes, and other tools are designed for soulwinning in **other lands** and for mass media **abroad**.

We practice what we preach.

World evangelism is top priority for us. It is our number one choice, the ministry nearest God's heart, the one thing Christ authorized every believer to share in.

When it is your **top priority**, you invest more in it than in anything else.

When it is your **top priority**, you allot more of your time to it than anything else — more of your energies, your plans, your efforts, your thoughts, your money, your very life.

World evangelism is top priority for us because it is the one way we can make sure that the blood of the unconverted will not be required at our hands.

I said this is **top priority for us** because we take it in a personal sense and because Christ includes every

Christian, every born-again child of God in His Great Commission.

It does no good to outline a fine doctrine or theory or proposition **unless it is personally expressed in a lifestyle**.

The Best Missionary Program

I lectured on **Giving To Missions** in a certain church. Afterwards, the pastor took me aside and said, "Dr. Osborn, you've changed me today. I never perceived gospel work abroad as a personal opportunity in my life. I expected that to be done by our foreign personnel. **I never realized that I could personally be a gospel messenger abroad even though I never went overseas myself.** I never realized that I could invest to sponsor a substitute or to send printed or recorded preachers on my behalf."

Then he added, "I always had a great deal of pride in my denomination's missionary program. I felt it was the best and bragged about it to others. It was not what I was doing, but what my denomination was doing, that I was proud of. I talked about **our** organization, **our** big program, **our** mission projects. I believed it was the best.

"But, Dr. Osborn, I confess to you that I never personally made any investment in missions. I put a small gift in the offering, but that was about all.

"Now I see that if every member of my organization did as I, we would have no soulwinning programs to talk about. It was a **denominational project** to me — not a **personal ministry**."

Our top priority is soulwinning.

Soulwinning is not reserved for missionaries, or preachers, or evangelists. **You and I can do it. It is our priority, our life, our passion.**

Christians have been inadvertently impressed that only professional clergy persons can serve as **ministers**.

But Christ dwells in **every** believer. **Every Christian is His witness. Every convert is His mouthpiece.** Christ wants to speak through **every believer who can talk or walk.** We are His witnesses! Millions who will not listen to the clergy will hear a genuine personal witness from a consecrated lay person.

With the tools we have available

today, any Christian can be a successful and happy witness for Christ.

Tote A Tool

An old man wept as he grasped my hand. Showing me his battered tape recorder, he said, "Dr. Osborn, you're my preacher. I carry you with me on tape from house to house, into hospitals, jails, and convalescent homes. I put you on that old machine and you preach for me. Then I pray for the listeners and they get saved and healed. Oh, how glad I am to be a soulwinner. Thank God, in my autumn years, I've learned to win souls."

Think what could be done if every believer would become a practical soulwinner.

We consider it our top priority to do everything we can to win souls. **We choose soulwinning. We think soulwinning. We dream about it. It is our passion, our zeal. It motivates us.**

As we yield our all to Christ Who is in us, we find our greatest joy in witnessing of Him because it is He Who is **at work within us**.

We keep remembering the extent to which God's love for us was proven. *His love is shed abroad in our hearts by the Holy Ghost* (Rom. 5:5), and we are inspired by the same passion that motivated Him.

Since our youth, we have dreamed of ways to witness for Christ. Those dreams became visions. Visions inspired us to prayer. Faith put action to those prayers. Soon those dreams became living, pulsating realities.

If People Could Have Read Our Minds

Years ago, we sat in Dr. Oswald J. Smith's missionary convention in Toronto, Canada, and dreamed of sending national foot soldiers to the frontiers of evangelism to extend the gospel to *the regions beyond.*

If people could have read our minds that day as we sat in The People's Church, they might have mocked us as youthful, emotional visionaries.

Other ministers listened to that tall, white-haired, aristocratic, missionary spokesman, Oswald J. Smith, as he shared the opportunity of world evangelism. They were impressed. They made notes on statistics. They admired his vision. But, few did anything about it.

However, that stately gentleman was building an unquenchable fire in the souls of this young couple. A new vision was being conceived. Soon the program of national evangelism was born and a new day dawned for sharing the gospel worldwide.

Pacesetters With Purpose

Since that day, no leader abroad has had to say, "We would reach the unreached of our areas, but we have no funds."

We have offered gospel leaders throughout the world funds to assist national preachers whom they will send as full-time messengers to the unreached.

We have already sponsored the gospel witness to over **130,000 previously unreached towns**, tribes, areas, or villages.

For several years, at least one new national church per day, opened and established this way, has become fully self-supporting so that our assistance

could be withdrawn. That is nearly four hundred new churches per year. This is not theory — **this principle works.**

Every arm of our world ministry is like that. First, it was a dream; then a vision; then prayer, faith, and action brought it forth as an outreach to millions of lost souls.

The starting point, however, is to believe enough in the scriptures and in the message of our Lord to dedicate oneself to share it with others. This motivates one to think and to dream of ways to win souls.

There are innumerable ideas for soul-winning which any believing Christian can implement.

I believe that any sincere Christian can do things that can be really effective to win lost souls. All thinkers are creators. All achievers in life are **dreamers, thinkers, planners** — then **doers**.

Some Criticize — Some Evangelize

People who get ideas and get things done are usually criticized. **Criticism accompanies success.** Critics usually dog the trail of achievers. **While some criticize, others evangelize.**

Those who succeed learn to never react to criticism. They adopt a positive attitude toward it. If we are reactionary, we will fight back to justify ourselves. When we do, we are predestined to lose. We will fail.

All those who are a success in life learn that criticism is really admiration in a subtle form. People usually only criticize the person who is out front. The failing, unsuccessful non-achieving person commands no attention and therefore draws no opposition.

Top priority for the successful person is to get the job done.

We have learned that if we set high goals and achieve them, critics may ridicule us outwardly, but inwardly they are challenged to become stronger, more daring, themselves.

We have learned that criticism is a cheap commodity, always plentiful, and certainly undeserving of our reaction.

There are two classes of people: those with **problems** and those with **solutions**. We choose to be people with solutions.

The person with solutions is the person in demand. Anybody can create problems, discuss them, analyze them, categorize them. Only the thinker — the creator, the achiever, the person of action — has solutions.

One of the best bits of advise we ever read was the statement: "Don't fight the problem; get on with the solution."

We have not spent our time holding conferences on how to win in evangelism. We have been getting on with the solution — spreading the gospel.

We have not been seeking out church leaders to discuss the problems which divide Christian workers. We have been getting on with the solution — cooperative soulwinning.

We have not only talked about the need for Christian literature. We have been supplying it. That is the solution.

We have not spent our time analyzing the problems of reaching the unreached. We have been applying the solution — sponsoring an army of gospel messengers and providing tons of soulwinning tools.

The enemies of the gospel have their eyes on the masses; but we do

**too, and we are doing something about
it — something that works!**

That is our policy: **Action.**

Not conventions, but **action**. Not theories, but **action**.

Not propositions, but **solutions**. Not
problems, but **answers**.

You can spend your life fighting the
problems involved in soulwinning. What
the world needs is ACTION.

It will cost you nothing to sit in on
group discussions, elaborating the problems of evangelism. That is why there are
always people available for committees.
You can always find plenty of people to
analyze the woes and complexities of a
problem.

But the one who has **solutions** must
pay dearly to serve humankind. **Solutions
cost money. They cost lives. They
demand dedication.**

Anyone can deliberate. We want to be
people with ideas for success.

The millions of unreached tribespeople are a problem. We are not interested
in theories or discussions. National evangelism is a **solution** that is working, so
we get on with it.

Our films are a **solution**. Millions are being reached through them, as with recorded audio and video gospel messages, mobile evangelism units, and tons of literature. We are getting on with **solutions**, not analyzing problems.

Commercial Tactics Become Talents

While in Africa, a pastor there showed us a commercial company which had a fleet of fifteen beautiful four-wheel-drive vehicles equipped to show secular films. They constantly canvassed the villages, gathering large crowds, showing films, and advertising their products. Then they made their sales. Out among the villages, their company was realizing attractive profits.

Some of the church leaders were bemoaning this problem. "Just think," they would say, "those villages are being reached with products like beer, cigarettes, liquor, etc. Yet we are not reaching them with the gospel."

I said to Daisy, "It will do no good to sit there and talk with those church leaders about this problem. **We can provide a solution.**"

Our new trans-world, mobile evangelism crusade was born. We began to
provide completely equipped mobile
evangelism units for active soulwinning
missions who were **going out after
the unreached.**

Since then, we have shipped overseas
more than a hundred large mobile units,
equipped with every tool we produce in
the language of the area, plus at least a
million tracts for each unit. **This is a
solution.**

The commercial world is doing it,
and we are too! The point is: **We are
DOING it. We are not just TALKING
about it.**

I would rather be placing my reputation on the block — **doing something
about soulwinning**, sending beautiful
van units to Christians engaged in evangelism in developing nations, than sitting
at home criticizing a program to **reach
the unreached.**

Whose Opinion Counts Most?

A famous statesman once said:

"It is not the critic who counts; not
the one who points out how the strong

person stumbled, or where the doer of deeds could have done better. The credit belongs to the one who is actually in the arena — in action — whose face is marred by dust and sweat and blood, who errs and comes short again and again; but who is spent in a worthy cause, who knows the triumph of high achievement — but who fails while daring greatly."

Yes, **criticism** and the inept persons who replenish it, abound. But **solutions** and the rare people who beget and apply them are valuable and scarce.

Critics come and go, rise and fall; but problem solvers are the pillars of society. It is not enough to bewail the sinfulness of this generation; **you and I have the solution.** We are **Christian witnesses**. We are **soulwinners**.

You can equip yourself with a supply of good gospel literature. Carry it with you and distribute it to people.

Get some good gospel audio cassettes. Invest a small amount and get yourself a cassette player. **Go out where the people are.** Be a witness for Christ.

Many Christian writers are producing excellent books, cassettes, and other tools for soulwinners.

Request a list of books, audio and video cassettes, films and our series of 18 special gospel tracts. They are available in many languages and have been proven effective worldwide.

We have produced these tools for soulwinners to help them be more successful. *We are laborers together with God* (1 Cor. 3:9).

We are soulwinners because we do not want the blood of sinners required at our hands.

Seed As You Breed

After you discover the joy of soulwinning in your own area or nation, plant some of the money God has entrusted you with to sponsor some tools for soulwinners **overseas**.

You can even sponsor a dozen audio cassette tapes in any of more than sixty major languages, for a national Christian worker to use in village evangelism, exactly as you learned to do at home among your people.

That way you will be involved in evangelism abroad and will share the

reward for every soul won by that national Christian witness.

Sponsor a quantity of literature for distribution in neglected villages.

Anointed messages on cassettes, books, and tracts will always be effective. They never tire, change their message, argue, become immoral, or compromise. They are among the best gospel messengers in the world. They will go as your substitutes.

Whatever has blessed you can bless so many others abroad, and you will share the reward for winning them to Christ.

It is not enough to just think or talk or pray about it. **Put action to your convictions.** Do something today while the fire is burning. Never let it go out. Stoke it, act on it, and it will blaze brighter.

When you have dedicated yourself to this top priority, then *if the unconverted turn not from their sinfulness, or from their sinful ways, they shall die in their iniquities; but you have delivered your soul.*

Tools for evangelism provided for soulwinning missions around the world has, for decades, been one of the proven outreaches of the Osborn ministries. (T. L. and Daisy, at center.)

10

This Century

We are soulwinners because of what we have experienced.

We have been conducting mass evangelism crusades for over three decades. In nearly seventy nations, the response has been the same.

Our most recent crusades have been the same as those conducted during our early ministry — the same strategy, the same messages, the same hunger, the same multitudes, the same miracles, the same results.

Even though we human beings come and go, the gospel is the same in any generation, when proclaimed in the power of the Holy Spirit.

Around the world, we have proven that **people of all races, religions, and creeds want to know God.** They have their forms of worship, their superstitions and their religions. But their spirits are not satisfied without Christ. They are ever searching for reality, unable to find the peace they seek. They pray in many different ways, but without answers.

They seek God but do not find Him.

Daisy and I have proven in almost 70 nations that once they have a chance to hear the gospel in simple language and —*in demonstration of the Spirit and of power* — **(1 Cor. 2:4), they almost stampede to receive Jesus Christ as Savior.**

In Nigeria, we never preached against their juju charms and fetishes which were hung around their legs, waists, arms, and necks. But as they learned of Christ and how to actually receive Him into their lives, they began plucking those things from their bodies and tossing them on the platform.

Burlap Bags of Charms

We carried large burlap bags of those charms and fetishes away from the campaign grounds and burned them, as Paul did. (See Acts 19:18-20.)

It was simple logic to those people: If the Son of the great creator God would come into their very own lives and dwell **with** them and **in** them, they did not need fetishes to protect them from evil spirits. Christ was enough.

We are soulwinners because of what we have experienced.

My wife and I went to India when we were only 21 years of age. There were few miracles in our ministry. We did not understand miracle faith. We led a few souls to Christ, but for the most part we failed.

When we preached Jesus Christ, Hindus kindly accepted Him in theory as another nice god to add to their others — but no change resulted in their lives.

Moslems reasoned: How do you know Jesus Christ is God's Son or that God raised Him from the dead?

They declared, "It is not true. He is dead. He was a good man, but was not God's Son — and certainly not risen from the dead."

They contended that the Koran was God's word and that Mohammed was His prophet.

We declared that the Bible was God's word and that Jesus Christ was His Son.

"Prove it, then." they said.

"We will. Look at these verses. Listen to what they say."

We began to read from our Bibles.

"Oh, no," they replied, "that is not God's word. That is no proof. This is God's word!" And they showed us their Koran.

The Bible or the Koran, **which was the word of God?**

How could we prove to them that the Bible was God's word? Without miracles we could not.

We returned to America, sick, discouraged and broken in spirit. But we never gave up. We fasted and prayed. We had seen the underprivileged masses. They needed Christ. We desired to win them. What was the answer?

Then Jesus Appeared

One morning at six o'clock, I was awakened as Jesus Christ stood in our bedroom. Looking upon Him, I lay there as one dead. I could not move a finger or a toe. Water ran from my eyes, though I was not conscious of weeping.

I do not know how long I gazed into His penetrating eyes before He disappeared, nor how long it was before I could move from my bed. I pulled myself onto the floor, face down, and lay prostrated before Him until the afternoon.

When I walked out of our room that day, I was a new man. I had met Jesus. He was not just a religion. He was alive and real. I saw Him. He became Lord of my life.

My attitude changed completely. Organizational leaders would never again be the primary influence in my life. Ambition to reach the top of the ladder in my church denomination was gone. To please Jesus became the passion of my life.

Since that day, what people say or think does not matter. I discovered the **living** Christ and He became **Lord** of my life.

Following that experience, a man of God came to our city, preaching and ministering to the sick. We witnessed hundreds of conversions and instant miracles of healing.

Ten thousand voices whirled over my head, saying, "You can do that. That's what Jesus did. That's what Peter and Paul did. That proves that Bible days are for today. That's the Bible way. You can do that."

I knew I could. That is, I knew Christ

could do it in and through me. I knew He had never changed.

So, we went after the unconverted.

We flew to Jamaica. In thirteen weeks over 9,000 souls accepted Christ; 90 totally blind people were healed; over 100 deaf mutes were restored. Hundreds of other miracles took place as the *Lord worked with us, confirming His word with signs following* (Mark 16:20).

Next, we went to Puerto Rico. The crusades were even greater. They were massive! Our message was simple. The people wanted reality. They believed when *they saw His miracles which he did on them that were diseased* (John 6:2).

Then we went to Haiti. It was the same again. Throngs too large for any building filled the yard, and even the roadway.

Next, it was Cuba. By that time, it began to look like more than just a spontaneous spiritual visitation in a couple of countries. It began to appear as a pattern.

The Sound of Tradition

These meetings had been heralded across the world.

But tradition is strong in the church.

Well-meaning ministers began to console us and to prepare us for inevitable failure. For surely, we were told, we must not expect such things to happen everywhere.

Some counseled us that from time to time, God foreordains these great events, but that it could not be a pattern.

We were told to be prepared for defeats as well as successes, that they would come because God just works that way, lest we become proud.

All of this sounded traditional to us, and we did not accept their words. We were convinced that the Great Commission which Jesus gave was for *every nation, to every creature.* He promised *these signs shall follow* those that believe and never mentioned an exception *unto the end of the world.*

We believed that any people in any nation in the whole world would believe **when they saw the miracles**. It seemed logical to us that **if we preached the gospel, Christ would confirm it with miracles.** We stood firm on this fact.

We were not prepared for failures

then, and we still are not. We believe in success. Christ never fails. His word never fails. The gospel never fails.

When we arrived in Cuba, spiritual leaders counseled us about the wisdom of balance and patience, that we should not necessarily expect a great meeting in Cuba just because of the successes we had experienced in Jamaica and Puerto Rico.

Their logic asserted that, "Jamaica was traditionally Christian already. Puerto Rico of course, was so influenced by the United States that religious opposition was not a factor there."

"But here in Cuba," they said, "the people are really religious. It may not be the same here."

People Are The Same

Despite these warnings, it turned out to be exactly the same.

An organized procession of a hundred religious leaders marched in the streets to warn the public against attending our mass crusade; but scores of thousands turned to the Lord and every Cuban crusade was massive.

Next, it was Venezuela. I still remember the counsel we received there:

"Oh, T.L. and Daisy, it's different here. In Cuba and Puerto Rico, religious opposition doesn't amount to much because the people are influenced by the United States, but here you are on the South American continent. You could be stoned to death."

Venezuela was exactly like Cuba. Multitudes believed. Thousands were saved. It was no different.

Then we traveled to Japan. When word was received that we were coming, many letters were rushed to us: "Don't come here. Japan is difficult. Miracles are not for this land. Japan seeks only academic enlightenment. They look to their ancestors as their spiritual source.

"Too many of her religions have healing cults. We Christians do not want our religion to be identified with these healers. Besides, miracles will never convince the Japanese about Jesus Christ."

Others said, "Japan is Buddhist and Shintoist. You are not accustomed to preaching to them. People in the western hemisphere are easy to reach. They already believe the Bible. They believe that Jesus is God's Son, that His blood was shed for our sins, but the Japanese would never believe this. You won't find it the same here. These people are not emotional. They will not respond."

The pattern of success in our crusades seemed to pose a threat to the very foundation of their church traditions in Japan.

At that time, it was unheard of to go to a nation, to preach in open public places, and to reap thousands of souls, again and again. It had to be emotionalism. The converts of this new mass evangelism could not last.

The early missionaries and church leaders never did it that way. They labored patiently for years to get a few converts — but their converts were thought to be solid, hand-picked, genuine.

No, this Osborn-style mass evangelism was superficial. It would never endure the test of time.

A pastor in India told me, "I've ministered here for five years and have never won a soul to Christ. That's the way it is in India. You must learn patience."

A revolutionary pattern seemed to be taking form. Instinctively, traditional minds reject anything new that threatens to replace instituted and accepted church policies and positions.

Buddhists And Shintoists

It seemed that God wanted to show His people everywhere that **there are no exceptions in gospel evangelism,** that His Great Commission would prove effective **wherever the gospel is proclaimed with living faith and action.**

Not all church leaders in Japan were pessimistic and negative. Some wrote, "Come over and help us too. **Modernism can never save the Japanese. They must see miracles!"**

I still recall the logic of a Baptist pastor who wrote: "Japan is full of phony healing cults. The Japanese must see the real thing. Our modern churches lack the miracle power. Come and help us. You have what we need to win this vast nation of people."

We accepted the challenge and Japan proved to be just like Jamaica, Cuba, and Venezuela. When they saw the miracles,

the Japanese screamed, wept, and re-
pented with more emotion than we had
ever seen anywhere yet.

We went to the historic and religious
heart of Japan — Kyoto. There on a large
field near the downtown area, thousands
heard the gospel. Forty-four deaf mutes
claimed healing in that one crusade.
Many great miracles were wrought.

Those Shintoists and Buddhists acted
just like Jamaicans or Cubans. Thousands
believed on Christ. The Japanese responded like any other people.

We went to Thailand — the strong
Buddhist monarchy of Southeast Asia.
Some said: "T.L. and Daisy, this won't
be like Japan. The Japanese Buddhists
have been influenced by the post-war
occupation. The Japanese are responsive
to Americans, but here in Thailand we
have the old-fashioned Buddhist. They
have never been ruled by a foreign power.
They will not listen to foreigners."

When we first ministered in Thailand,
there were less than a dozen people in
the entire country who had received an
apostolic baptism of the Holy Spirit.
Even they were not enthusiastic about

proclaiming the gospel out in public places. This would violate Thai culture.

Such an approach would seem too aggressive for any Thai community. They are a very serene and sensitive people. Any approach to them must be in keeping with their traditional poise.

Needless to say, when the Thai people witnessed that the blind see, the cripples walk, the lepers cleansed, and the deaf hear, their response was no different than the Japanese, the Venezuelans, the Cubans, the Puerto Ricans, or the Jamaicans. They received the living Christ and enthusiastically began to follow Him.

Today, there are thousands of Spirit-filled Christians all over Thailand. Great soulwinning ministries have flourished there, building strong, big churches.

When we first ministered in Java, Indonesia, the population was 95% Moslem. Around the world we had heard how difficult the Moslems were to reach. They do not believe that Jesus is God's Son or that God raised Him from the dead. We remembered how helpless we were to convince them in India. However, by the time we reached the capital city on the island of Java, things were different. We knew how to believe for miracles.

The first night that I preached to the multitude, I did something unusual at the end of the message.

I told them that I would not expect them to accept Jesus Christ unless He proved Himself alive by undeniable miracles. I expressed my feelings that a dead Christ could do them no good.

I emphasized the fact that Jesus Christ was confirmed by miracles 2,000 years ago; that if He is alive today, then God would confirm this fact by doing undeniable miracles in their presence.

They knew about the historical Jesus. They had heard that He was a good man, even a prophet with healing powers to do miracles. They knew that He had been crucified, and they were convinced that the Christian teaching of His resurrection was false.

There is only one message for a Moslem: If Jesus Christ is alive, let Him do the miracles which He did before He was killed. If He is dead, He **cannot.** If He is risen, He **will**.

I called for deaf people. I told them I would pray in Jesus' name. If Christ is dead, His name would have no power. If He is alive, He would do the same as He did before He died on the cross.

A Moslem Priest First

The first man to be prayed for was a Moslem priest about 55 years old wearing his black fez, indicating he had been a pilgrim to the revered Moslem city of Mecca in Arabia.

He was born totally deaf in one of his ears and had never heard a sound from that ear.

I witnessed to him of Jesus Christ, then told him how I would pray. I explained that God was looking down on us. I witnessed to him that God had raised His Son from the dead. I explained that God wanted people to know that Christ is alive and would therefore give proof of His resurrection from the dead by doing this miracle.

Then I told the audience: "If this man does not hear when I have finished praying, you can say I am a false preacher and Jesus is dead. But if he does hear,

you will know that Christ is risen, because a dead Christ cannot do such a
miracle."

I looked at him and said, "That it
may be known that Jesus Christ is God's
Son, that God raised Him from the dead,
that only through Him and His shed
blood can we come to God and receive
eternal life; let this be known according
to the scripture by causing this deaf ear
to hear, in Jesus Christ's name. Amen!"

Missions With Miracles

The entire audience gasped when the
Moslem priest could hear the faintest
whisper and even the ticking of a watch.

Thousands raised their hands that
night indicating their desire to accept
Jesus Christ as their Savior. How different this was from the embarrassment we
had suffered in trying to convince
Moslems in India seven years earlier.

The Moslems were just like the
Japanese **when they saw the proof of
the gospel of Jesus Christ.**

**Christianity without miracles can-
not prove that Jesus is alive.** Take miracles out of Christianity and all you have

left is another lifeless religion.

Moslems know their prophet Mohammed is dead, but we know our prophet Jesus is alive. When that is proven by miracles, people forsake the dead prophet and follow One who is alive. Without miracles, there is no proof.

This is why Jesus commissioned every believer to preach to all the world, promising that supernatural signs would follow — **among all nations, unto the end of the world.** He knew it would always require miracles to really show the world that Jesus is alive.

When we were in India as young missionaries, Moslems challenged us: "Prove that your Christ lives!"

We were helpless and embarrassed. We had to leave — or settle down to the status quo of faithfulness and patience, without results. We could not bring ourselves to do that.

But in Indonesia, it was different.

One evening in that great campaign, a young Moslem priest — a real fanatic, started up the platform steps in anger, to interrupt me while I was preaching. My wife, Daisy, spotted him coming and intercepted him at the steps.

He said, "That man is false. Jesus is dead. He is not God's Son. Let me speak to the people about Mohammed, God's true prophet."

Daisy tried to reason with him, but he was too emotional.

Finally, she told him, "Listen, I'm a Christian and here's what I will do. I will interrupt my husband on one condition: you and I will go together to the microphone. We will not argue. We will show which prophet is true and alive by calling for someone totally blind to come forward.

"You pray for him, in the presence of the people, and in the name of Mohammed. If he sees, we will believe on your prophet.

"If no miracle results, then I'll pray for him in the name of Jesus. If he sees, then you and your people will know that what the Bible says about Christ is true — that He is God's Son and that God has raised Him from the dead to be the Savior of the world."

The young Moslem priest refused the

challenge by Daisy. He turned away and left in a rage.

This was what we could not do in India as young missionaries.

We finally experienced the joy of returning to India, fourteen years later after we had so miserably failed there. We went back to the same university city of Lucknow, where we had been unable to prove to the Hindus and Moslems that Jesus Christ is the living, resurrected Son of God, the Savior of the world.

This time we were different! 20,000 to 40,000 people massed in front of the big stadium grounds.

We preached that *Jesus Christ is the same yesterday, today and forever.* Then we prayed. The deaf heard. Cripples walked. Blind people received sight. Lepers were cleansed. Thousands accepted Christ.

Jesus was showing Himself to India through us. Our search for Truth had paid off. This is the way world evangelism was meant to be carried out.

Christ showed himself alive by many infallible proofs (Acts 1:3).

The Hooked Hindu

A young Hindu, a university student, stood out in the multitude, ridiculing everything. When we prayed, Jesus Christ suddenly appeared to him, dressed in a purple robe. He opened His nail-pierced hands and extended them to the young man, and as He did, He spoke these words:

"Behold my hands, I am Jesus."

The youth fell to the ground — weeping, repenting, sobbing. Then he rushed to the microphone and with tears bathing his face he told what he had seen and urged his people to believe on Jesus.

How different than it had been in our meetings fourteen years earlier! With miracles, India was the same as other nations.

How Did It Happen?

Next, it was Africa where, again, we proved that people are the same everywhere.

A Moslem beggar in Africa, paralyzed by polio, had crawled on the ground for thirty years. He dragged himself in the dirt until he reached the crusade. He listened to the gospel and as he believed on Jesus Christ, he was instantly healed. He pushed through the crowd and walked up before the multitude to show himself and the miracle he had received, to the people.

As he stood on the platform in tears, he cried out: "Jesus Christ must be alive. Otherwise, how could He have healed me? Mohammed is dead, but Jesus lives. Look at me. You know me. I have begged in your streets. Now I can walk. Look! This Jesus lives!"

What greater sermon could be preached than that? It sounded like the book of Acts being re-enacted in our day.

Around the world we have seen that people want Christ. They seek reality and they believe, when they have proof that Jesus is alive and real.

God made all human beings alike. People are made to walk with God. They instinctively seek for Him. This is why every unevangelized tribe practices some kind of religious ritual in search of God.

The gospel, straightforward and in simple terms — not explained, but proclaimed — *is the power of God unto salvation to everyone that believeth* (Rom. 1:16).

People want the gospel. And our task is to preach it, witness of it, tell it, confess it everywhere — to crowds or to individuals, in public places or in private homes. People want what we have. We have proven this worldwide. **This is why we are soulwinners.**

Europe No Different

The cynic may say, "Ah, that's true among the people in the developing nations, but not in the industrialized world!"

One of the greatest crusades we ever conducted, where the audiences numbered over 150,000 people in a single meeting, was in the capitol city of orthodox, traditional, Christian Holland.

Culture has reached no greater peak anywhere than in sophisticated Europe. Yet when they saw the miracles, multiplied thousands of them were saved for the first time in their lives. It has proven to be the same all over Europe, Great Britain and North America.

You see, there are only two kinds of preachers or Christian workers: negative and positive — doubters and believers.

Some think that if they preach on the streets, no one will listen and passers-by will scoff at them; that any literature they distribute will only be thrown on the ground and trod upon; that doors will be shut in their faces. That is a negative attitude about a very positive opportunity.

We believe that when we preach on the streets, crowds will gather around us, straining to hear our message; that passers-by will be delighted to see a Christian out witnessing.

We believe that when we distribute gospel literature, it will be eagerly received, treasured, and read.

We believe that when we knock on doors, we will find families who welcome our help, sick people who need healing, problems which need solutions, hearts and ears open to the counsel and prayers of a real dedicated Christian who has living faith. This is the positive approach, and it works.

We are soulwinners and we have proven around the world, in every conceivable circumstance, that people want Christ. They long for God, for His salvation, for eternal life. They are made in God's image to be like Him, to walk and talk with Him. They are never content until they find Jesus Christ who is the Way, the Truth, and the Life. (See John 14:6.)

With sixty million unreached people being added to our generation every year — people seeking for light and life — our priority is to witness, preach the gospel, to produce soulwinning tools for Christians. This is our priority — until Christ returns. **This is the seventh reason we are soulwinners.**

Outbreak in Soulwinning

We first published these *Seven Reasons Why We Are Soulwinners* in our magazine FAITH DIGEST. This magazine has gone to hundreds of thousands of Christians and gospel ministers in over 130 nations.

From around the world, letters poured

into our offices acclaiming this series as the most challenging on soulwinning yet presented. Hundreds of believers, preachers, missionaries and national leaders have rededicated themselves to **reach out after the unconverted** with a fresh passion for soulwinning.

Tens of thousands of Christians are taking gospel literature, anointed messages on cassettes, and other soulwinning tools out into markets, streets, homes, jails, and hospitals. They are active in face-to-face evangelism, praying for the sick and leading the unconverted to Christ **right out where they are!**

This is what the early church did and this is what is happening again in this century — among those who really believe the Gospels and the book of Acts.

This is what we are encouraging believers to do around the world — to become soulwinners.

This is why I have written this soulwinning book. It is producing fresh motivation in the lives of thousands of Christians worldwide.

Because we know people want Christ — because we have proven it

worldwide — we are soulwinners.

I believe that a fresh passion for souls has developed in you as you have read this book. New ideas and new possibilities are before you now. I believe that now, you will go out and let Christ witness **through you — out where the people are**.

Go then and tell them of Christ. You will be choosing the lifestyle that guarantees success, happiness and real fulfillment.

Soulwinning is the greatest opportunity on earth. Tools are available to you, so let them open the door to a fresh new ministry of reaching people, not only in your area but everywhere that new possibilities are available to you.

Osborn Crusade — Calabar

Tens of thousands of gospel messages in 67 languages are provided by the Osborn Ministries, for Soulwinning outreaches worldwide.

11
You Are God's Connection

Jesus preached perhaps His greatest sermons to individuals — to Nicodemus, to the woman at the well.

Philip made a missionary journey into the desert and preached his greatest sermon to an individual. (See Acts 8:26-29.) Hundreds of years later when missionaries crossed the desert into Ethiopia, they found the entire country had been opened to the gospel — the result of witnessing to one individual.

Paul delivered one of his greatest and most persuasive sermons to an individual, Felix the governor, and almost persuaded him to be a Christian.

No preacher, no Christian, is fully successful until he masters the secrets of leading a person to Christ.

Yet, all too often, church members who really want to serve the Lord and desire to win souls are not involved because they do not know how or where to begin. They have not realized that **the individual Christian is the church —**

Christ's body — through which He continues ministering and witnessing today.

To help you begin, take advantage of many tools for soulwinners which are available from so many good sources. Once you gain confidence, nothing will ever stop you from leading people to Christ.

One couple brought 129 new people to their own church within two years because they went out witnessing as a regular part of their Christian living.

What would happen in your church if 25 members became systematic soulwinners? It would revolutionize your church or any other. So do it. Start now. When you begin and start to testify of your thrilling experiences, others will follow. Soon, you can be the cause of a fresh new revival in your church. (Our book, *Join This Chariot*, shows you, step by step, how to lead a soul to Christ.)

While you stand and chat with a friend, while you read a newspaper, while you sleep at night — every minute of every day — at least 80 souls slip beyond the barriers of time into eternity.

This is why we encourage Christians

to be soulwinners. Before you go to church **alone**, before you pray at your church altar, before you give your tithes and offerings, before you send your world evangelism investment — just think: over 80 people a minute, over 80 a minute, over 80 a minute. And most of them have never heard the gospel, **even once**.

You cannot reach all of them, but you can reach some. So begin. You can do it. You are Christ's body — His feet, His arms, His lips, His voice. He can only reach lost souls through people like you.

Jesus chose business people, laboring, ordinary people such as fishermen and tax collectors to be His witnesses.

On the day of Pentecost, 120 ordinary individuals were filled with the Holy Ghost to be Christ's witnesses. (See Acts 1:8; 2:4.) They were not professionals with degrees.

Persecution forced the early Christians to spread out from Jerusalem. Only the Apostles remained. *They that were scattered abroad went everywhere preaching the word* (Acts 8:4).

Who were scattered? Lay people, not apostles. The laity *went everywhere preaching the word.*

The first martyr, Stephen, was a layman.

The first evangelist, Philip, was a layman.

The true church is a lay movement — not an organization dominated by professionals; but individual believers in whom Christ is born.

God has placed you where you are in life to be His contact there! The preacher cannot reach your contacts. You are there — among your classmates, in your factory, in your neighborhood. **You** are God's connection with those around you. **You** are His voice, His body.

Be His witness. Let Him speak **through** you. Anyone who truly knows Christ, **has something to say**. The one who has nothing to say probably does not really know Christ personally.

Your church needs your witness if it is to be a soulwinning church. Most of all, **the great shepherd depends on your body as His soulwinning instrument, as the soulwinning church in action.**

You have a personal testimony. Share it with those you meet. That would be "THE

GOSPEL ACCORDING TO Y-O-U."

Christian soulwinning. Here is the case in a nutshell:

1. Your Calling: Every Believer A Witness.

Christian means Christlike.

Christ was the greatest soulwinner. He came to seek and save the lost.

He told His **first** followers to be *fishers of people* and His **last** followers to witness to *every creature*.

To be Christlike (a Christian) is to be a soulwinner — to be Christ inhabited.

Most Christians want to witness, but are timid and do not know how. They do not know that they are Christ's body.

2. Your Field: Out Where the People Are.

Reach the unchurched, the down-and-outers, the non-Christians. They will listen. They need you.

The unconverted do not go to church. Christ can never reach them except **through people like you**.

Street corners, houses, stores, slums, bedsides, marketplaces, beaches, jails, hospitals, resorts, fairs, clubs, door to door — **among the unconverted and the**

unchurched — that is the darkness where Christ's light in your life will shine brightest.

Lead them to Christ. Let Him speak to them through your lips. They will follow you to your church to receive more light.

3. Your Goal: Adding To Your Church.

It is not enough to witness or win souls. They should be influenced into a church where a faithful pastor can establish them in Bible faith.

Stamp every piece of literature you distribute with your church name and address. Welcome new contacts to your congregation. Meet them there. Introduce them to fellow Christians — and to your pastor.

Do follow up ministry. Visit them. Give them good literature. Remind them of church meetings. Do not stop until they have been added to your church.

4. Your Tools: Effective Gospel Literature.

We offer 18 different Christ centered tracts. Soulwinners may obtain them in quantities for a reasonable price. They have been provided by the millions for church leaders and national Christians all over the free world.

Carry them wherever you go. These **paper preachers**, written in common language for the person on the street, will witness for you.

Imprinted with your church name and address, each tract speaks for your church.

Request information about them today. Use them for your personal witnessing, to help you lead new souls to Christ.

Gospel Cassettes

Almost anywhere, you can buy a portable, transistorized, battery powered cassette player with a microphone. This is a marvelous tool for witnessing to groups as well as to individuals.

Then with a set of our crusade cassettes (or any of innumerable others), you can extend the influence and power of these great crusades and other ministries to individuals and groups in your own church area, or wherever you have influence.

Such a unit makes you an effective

witness to reach more souls and to draw them into your church or Bible group for more instructions on how to follow Christ.

Faith Books

We have written several books, which contain the cream of our teachings on evangelism, self-esteem, salvation, healing, faith and soulwinning. They are easy to read — direct and to the point.

They make a powerful faith library — a compact Bible school for soulwinners.

Each book bears a clear salvation message and is a faith builder. They are ideal tools to give or loan to the sick, the unbeliever, the shut-in, or to a neighbor as a follow-up to your witness. It will anchor their faith and draw them into your home church. (Write for a complete list.)

Reaching the Unchurched

Without a vision, the people perish (Prov. 29:18).

Keep your vision fresh by reading our world evangelism news magazine, FAITH DIGEST. It is a family favorite among

Christians in 130 nations. It is FREE upon request.

It contains new ideas and fresh concepts to build your faith and inspire you to win more souls and lead them into your congregation.

T. L. & Daisy Osborn have shared their SOULWINNING principles and vision with tens of thousands of national preachers worldwide, such as this soulwinning institute they conducted in E. Africa.

T. L. Osborn uses "talking box" to give a gospel witness to this Papua-New Guinea villager in his own native dialect.

12
Where No Voice Can Speak

Every Christian who wants to win souls to Christ should learn the power and the effectiveness of witnessing with the printed page.

For over three decades, we have prayerfully worked at the answer to the question: How can the world be evangelized within one generation?

There is a way.

After travel and extensive ministry in nearly seventy countries, we have proven beyond doubt that one of the most effective ways to carry out the Great Commission of Christ is by means of the printed page.

We have heard the saying, "The pen is mightier than the sword." This is true. It is equally true that the pen is mightier than the human voice.

The written word can go where the human voice cannot go.

It has no passport or visa problem.

It travels economically.

It leaps language barriers and is never influenced by racial prejudice.

It can sail the oceans, trek the deserts, and trudge the jungle footpaths of every continent on earth.

It can penetrate the crowded cities and reach the sparsely settled countryside, entering sophisticated mansions and village cottages alike.

It can tell its story in home or shop, in the factory or in the field.

It can even penetrate the forgotten areas where people are too poor or primitive to have access to radio or TV. In areas where reception is practically nil because of mountain ranges or rugged peaks and foul weather, **printed preachers** find their way.

The written word is often more powerful than the human voice. They even said of the Apostle Paul, *His letters are weighty and powerful, but his bodily presence is weak, and his speech contemptible* (2 Cor. 10:10).

The written word knows no fear and flinches in the face of no person.

It preaches the same message to the rich and to the poor, to the king and to the commoner.

It never loses its temper and never

retaliates in anger.

It pays no attention to scoffs, jeers, or insults.

It never tires, but witnesses 24 hours a day, even while we sleep.

It is never discouraged, but will tell its story over and over again.

It will speak to one as willingly as to a multitude, to a multitude as readily as to one.

It always catches a person in just the right mood to be receptive, for it only speaks as one chooses to listen.

It can be received, read, and studied in secret.

It gets undivided attention in the quiet hours.

It speaks without a foreign accent.

The written word is more permanent than the human voice.

It never compromises and never changes its message.

It continues to speak and make its message plain, long after audible words have been forgotten and their sound has faded.

It continues to witness and influence long after its author has died. The works of Luther, Calvin, and Knox are still being circulated after more than 400 years. And think of the Bible itself — what a graphic illustration of the power and permanence of the printed page.

Would you like to win souls?

If you are an average, healthy Christian, your answer is, "Yes."

Well, there are souls to be won, and you can win them. Only a small percentage of Christians can be full-time workers, evangelists, pastors, missionaries, teachers, or writers; but **every believer can win people through the printed page.**

Peter Cartwright, the famous circuit rider and pioneer evangelist, said, "For more than fifty years I have firmly believed it is part and parcel of a Christian's sacred duty to circulate religious literature. The religious press is destined, under the order of providence, to minister salvation's grace to the perishing millions of the earth."

We have shared that attitude for many years. A veritable river of literature has been pouring from our offices to all corners of the earth in over 120 dialects and languages. Millions of copies have been published each month.

There are two ways you can share in soulwinning:

First, you can pray. Pray that God's blessings will rest upon the dedicated workers who carefully and prayerfully distribute the **printed preachers.** (You can distribute them, too.) Pray that every tract or book will be good seed sown upon *good ground,* and that it will bring forth a bountiful harvest.

Second, you can share by sponsoring the publication of millions of gospel tracts in languages around the world.

"It is urgent that we saturate all nations with Christian literature," says a noted authority on the methods used in atheistic propaganda to dominate public opinion. "I know of no other project so desperately necessary or one that will pay such rich dividends in winning souls."

In nearly seventy countries, I have seldom seen a person toss aside a gospel tract. I have seen them fight over them many times when there were not enough for everyone to have one.

Millions of hands are reaching to us

for these printed morsels of the bread of Life. We are filling those hands, around the world, to the extent of our means.

May God grant that you, too, will become a preacher to millions through the power of the printed page.

13
The Real Christian

Now I present this last chapter to you if you are not sure about your own salvation, or not certain that you have really been born again, or if you do not know if you are a real Christian, or if you have simply accepted a religion, joined a church and mentally assented to the Bible, without experiencing the new birth.

Most of all, I present this chapter to you who have never been saved or converted and know it.

The Bible says that we can *know that we have passed from death unto life* (1 John 3:14).

This chapter will help you to know, beyond a doubt, that you have experienced this inner miracle. It will take place in you while you read this with reverence and simple faith.

If you are already a Christian, committed to winning souls, this chapter can serve as a guide to help you show others how to experience the miracle of the new birth.

I want to tell you how you can be saved from hell, saved from your sins, saved from death, saved from disease, saved from evil.

You can be saved right now.

The Bible says, *This is a faithful saying, and worthy of all acceptation, that Christ Jesus came into the world to save sinners* (1 Tim. 1:15).

The Bible says, *God sent not His Son into the world to condemn the world; but that the world through Him might be saved* (John 3:17).

Peter said, *Whoever shall call on the name of the Lord shall be saved* (Acts 2:21).

You can be saved today. This is what you need: to be saved, to know Jesus Christ as your personal Savior.

But what does it mean to be **saved**?

First: To be **saved** means to be born again, to become a child of God.

Jesus said, *You must be born again* (John 3:7). This is a miracle. Christ actually enters your life, and you are made new because He begins to live in you. This is not accepting a religion. This is accepting Christ. He is a person, not a philosophy. He is reality, not theory.

When I was married and accepted Daisy as my wife, I did not get the marriage religion. I received a person — Daisy, as my wife.

When I was saved by receiving Christ, I did not get the Christian religion. I received a Person, the Lord Jesus. My conversion was as definite an experience as was my marriage. On both occasions, I received another person into my life.

The Bible says, *As many as received Him, to them gave He power to become the children of God* (John 1:12).

What a marvel that one can receive a new birth and be born into God's royal family. You have been born once — born in sin, a child of sin, a servant of the devil. Now Christ says, *You must be born again* (John 3:7). You must be converted — be saved, changed, made new.

Second: To be **saved** means to have your sins forgiven.

The Bible says, *He forgives all your iniquities* (Ps. 103:3).

The angel said, *You shall call His name JESUS: for he shall save His people from their sins* (Matt. 1:21).

God says, *I am He that blots out your transgressions* (Is. 43:25). *And their sins and iniquities will I remember no more* (Heb. 10:17).

As far as the east is from the west, so far has He removed our transgressions from us (Ps. 103:12).

Third: To be **saved** means to receive a new spiritual life.

Paul says, *If any one be in Christ, that person is a new creature: old things are passed away; behold all things are become new* (2 Cor. 5:17).

That is exactly what happens when Christ saves you. A conversion takes place. Old desires, habits, and diseases pass away. All things become new. You receive a new life, a new nature, new health, new desires, new ambitions. You receive Christ's life.

He said, *I am come that they might have life, and that they might have it more abundantly* (John 10:10).

Fourth: To be **saved** means to receive

peace.

Jesus said, *Peace I leave with you. My peace I give unto you* (John 14:27). He said, *I have spoken unto you, that in me you might have peace* (John 16:33).

Real peace only comes with Christ's pardon and salvation. In sin you can never have peace in your soul. The Bible says, *There is no peace, says my God, to the wicked* (Is. 57:21). But *being justified by faith, we have peace with God through our Lord Jesus Christ* (Rom. 5:1).

Fifth: To be **saved** means to have fellowship with God.

You were created in God's likeness, so you could walk and talk with Him. But your sins separated you from God. Now, instead of fellowship with the Father, you fear God. The thought of facing Him frightens you. Your sin condemns you and creates in you a sense of guilt before God.

Only Christ can save you from your sins. He will blot out every stain and bring you back to God with a clean record — as if you had never sinned. Then you can say with the apostle John:

Truly our fellowship is with the Father, and with His Son Jesus Christ (1 John 1:3).

He will be *a friend that sticks closer than a brother or sister* (Prov. 18:24).

No person was made for a life of sin and disease. You were created to walk with God. But sin separated you from God.

Your iniquities have separated between you and your God, and your sins have hid His face from you, that He will not hear (Is. 59:2).

But, His blood was shed for many, *for the remission of sins* (Matt. 26:28).

If we confess our sin (to Him), *He is faithful and just to forgive us our sins, and to cleanse us from all unrighteousness* (1 John 1:9).

John said, *We know that we have passed from death unto life* (1 John 3:14). There are many things in this world which you may never know, but you can know you have Christ's life in you. You can know that you have been saved — that you are born again.

To say, "I don't know for sure if I'm

saved," is like a husband or a wife saying, "I don't know for sure if I'm married."

To say, "I think I'm saved. I try to be, but I'm not sure about it," is like saying, "I think I'm married. I try to be, but I'm not sure about it."

Jesus said, *One who believes* (the gospel) *and is baptized shall be saved* (Mark 16:16).

Paul said, *If you shall confess with your mouth the Lord Jesus, and shall believe in your heart that God has raised Him from the dead, you shall be saved* (Rom. 10:9).

These scriptures promise: *You shall be saved.*

Follow them, do what they say, and you can know that you have received Christ — that you have passed from death unto life, that you are saved! This is not accepting a religion. This is Christianity — the Christ life!

What is a **real** Christian?

According to the Bible, a real Christian is a person who:

1. Has come to God as a lost sinner;

2. Has accepted by faith the Lord Jesus Christ as personal Savior by surrendering to Him as Lord and Master;

3. Has confessed Christ as Lord before the world;

4. Is striving to please Him in everything, every day.

If you are not sure that you have personally accepted Jesus Christ into your heart as your Lord and Master, then follow these seven steps prayerfully:

First: Realize that you are a sinner.

All have sinned, and come short of the glory of God (Rom. 3:23).

If we say that we have no sin, we deceive ourselves (1 John 1:8).

Second: Truly be sorry for and repent of your sins.

And the publican, standing afar off, would not lift up so much as his eyes unto heaven, but smote upon his breast, saying, God be merciful to me a sinner (Luke 18:13).

For godly sorrow works repentance to salvation (2 Cor. 7:10).

Third: Confess your sins to God.

One who covers sin shall not prosper: but whoever confesses and forsakes them shall have mercy (Prov. 28:13).

If we confess our sins (to Him), *He is faithful and just to forgive us our sins, and to cleanse us from all unrighteousness* (1 John 1:9).

Fourth: Forsake your sins, or put them away.

Let the wicked forsake their way, and the unrighteous their thoughts; and let them return unto the Lord, and He will have mercy upon them ... for He will abundantly pardon (Is. 55:7).

Whoever confesses and forsakes sin shall have mercy (Prov. 28:13).

Fifth: Ask forgiveness for your sins.

Who forgives all your iniquities (Ps. 103:3).

Come now, and let us reason together, says the Lord: though your sins be as scarlet, they shall be white as snow; though they be red like crimson, they shall be as wool (Is. 1:18).

Sixth: Consecrate your entire life to Christ.

Whoever shall confess me before others, I will confess also before my Father which is in heaven (Matt. 10:32).

But you are a chosen generation ...

that you should show forth the praises of Him who has called you out of darkness into His marvelous light (1 Pet. 2:9).

Seventh: Believe that God saves you by His grace.

For by grace are you saved through faith; and that not of yourselves; it is the gift of God: not of works, let any one should boast (Eph. 2:8,9).

Accept Christ Now

Now is the day of salvation, says 2 Corinthians 6:2. Not some other day — but now, this very day!

Behold, now is the accepted time (2 Cor. 6:2). Not some other time — but right now!

Seek the Lord while He may be found, call upon him while He is near: Let the wicked forsake their ways, and the unrighteous their thoughts: and let them return unto the Lord, and He will have mercy upon them ... for He will abundantly pardon (Is. 55:6,7).

The Lord is near you this very moment, so before you put down this book, if you have not yet accepted Jesus

Christ as your personal Savior, find a place alone with God where you will not be disturbed. Get on your knees and pray to the Lord this prayer right out loud:

—Dear Lord, I come before You to receive the gift of God which is eternal life. I acknowledge that I have sinned against You. I confess all of my sins to You, here and now.

I am sorry for my sins which have separated me from Your blessing, and I truly repent and ask Your forgiveness.

I believe on Your Son, Jesus Christ. I believe that, in Your great mercy and love, You sent Him to die for me, in my place. I believe He rose from the dead to live forever as my Savior.

I do, here and now, welcome Jesus Christ into my heart as my Savior from sin, from hell, and from all the power of the devil. I accept Christ as Lord of my life. Here and now, I devote my life to pleasing You.

Jesus Christ, You have said that, if I will come to You, You will in no wise cast me out. I have come to You with all my heart, seeking salvation and trusting only in Your blood. I am sure that You do not reject me.

You have said, "If I will confess with my mouth the Lord Jesus, and shall believe in my heart that God has raised Him from the dead, I shall be saved" (Rom. 10:9).

I believe with all my heart that You are my Lord, risen from the dead. I do, here and now, confess You as my Master, my Savior, my Lord. I receive You now into my heart by faith.

Because You died for me, suffering the penalty which I ought to have suffered, I know my sins can never condemn me again. You paid the full price for my redemption.

Your Word says, "As many as received (Jesus Christ), to them gave He power to become the children of God" (John 1:12).

I believe that You do at this very moment give me power to become Your child. I believe that You forgive me now. Your precious blood washes all my sins away. You were wounded for my transgressions. You were bruised for my iniquities. The punishment I ought to have endured was laid upon You.

I know I am forgiven.

Thank You, Lord!

From this hour, I will read Your word and do my best to follow You and to please You in all that I think and do and say. I am now a real Christian, a representative of Jesus Christ on earth.

Now I know I am saved.

Amen!—

Daisy and I love you. God loves you and values you. Experience LIFE, HAPPINESS, HEALTH and DIGNITY as you GO WITH GOD and REALLY LIVE.

As an act of faith, register your decision by signing your name in the decision box that follows.

MY DECISION

Today I have read this chapter on **The Real Christian**. I have learned what it means to be saved. I have sincerely taken the seven steps outlined here and have reverently prayed the prayer.

I believe I have received Jesus Christ in my own life. I am now a New Creature. I commit my life to do my best to please God in all that I think and say and do. With His grace and help, I shall share Jesus Christ with others.

Relying on Him to keep me by His grace, I have made this decision today, in Jesus' name.

Signed _____

Date _____

Seal your decision and confession by writing us a personal letter to tell us that you have accepted Jesus Christ and that you have received the inner miracle of conversion.

We pray for every person who reads this book. Our greatest reward is to receive letters from those who have been saved as a result.

We will answer you personally, and we shall then become prayer partners in following and serving Jesus Christ.

Write us today, lest you forget. Tell us, in your own words, what took place.

We are praying for you.

— T. L. Osborn

Osborn Crusade — Embu

JESU KRISTO ATUURAGA ATEKUGARURUKA,
IRA, NA UMUTHI, O'NA ... 'ENE NA'TENE

The Osborn World Ministry

The ministry of T. L. and Daisy Osborn has made an unprecedented impact on the world in our time. They are valued among the great soulwinners of this century.

Married at ages 17 and 18, the Osborns were missionaries in India at 20 and 21. In 1949 they instituted the Osborn Foundation — a world evangelism and missionary church organization.

Their **life commitment**: To express and propagate the gospel of Jesus Christ to people throughout the world.

Their **guiding principle**: The top priority of the church is the evangelization of the world.

Their **motto**: **One Way — Jesus**; **One Job — Evangelism**

The Osborns have conducted mass crusades in nearly 70 nations, preaching to audiences ranging from 10,000 to 200,000 nightly.

They have sponsored over 20,000 national preachers as full-time missionaries, reaching their own tribes and villages.

They have published gospel literature in 132 languages and dialects.

They have produced documentary films and crusade tapes for public evangelism in 65 languages.

They have provided airlifts and huge shipments of soulwinning tools for gospel missions and workers worldwide.

They have furnished vehicles with films, projectors, screens, generators, P.A. systems, audio cassettes and cassette players, and great quantities of literature for evangelism abroad.

T. L. Osborn is an energetic and prolific writer whose books have helped stimulate today's worldwide miracle-evangelism awakening. His living classic, *Healing the Sick* — now in its 27th edition — has been a faith-building best-seller since 1951.

The Osborns' team effort in world evangelism is unequalled as they proclaim the Good News to the world: that *Jesus Christ is the same yesterday, today and forever* (Heb. 13:8).

***